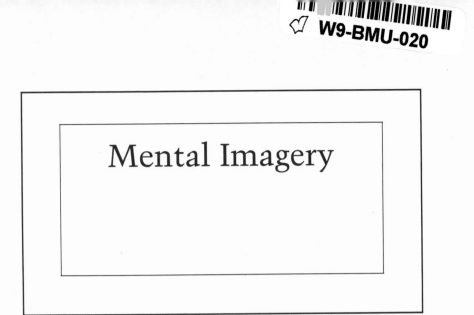

Mental Imagery

Mental Imagery

On the Limits of Cognitive Science

MARK ROLLINS

Yale University Press   New Haven & London

Designed by Richard Hendel
and set in Trump type
by Brevis Press, Bethany, Connecticut.
Printed in the United States of America by
BookCrafters, Chelsea, Michigan.

Library of Congress Cataloging-in-Publication Data
Rollins, Mark, 1947–
Mental imagery : on the limits of cognitive science / Mark
Rollins.
p. cm.
Bibliography: p.
Includes index.
ISBN 0–300–04491–7 (cloth)
0–300–05472–6 (pbk.)
1. Imagery (Psychology) 2. Cognition. 3. Cognitive science.
I. Title.
BF367.R65 1989 88–36541
153.3'2—dc19 CIP

10 9 8 7 6 5 4 3 2

TO CYNTHIA

Contents

Acknowledgments

There are a number of people whose advice and encouragement have been of great help in the writing of this book. In particular, I owe a substantial debt to Arthur Danto, who read early versions of the work and with whom I have continued to have many valuable discussions. His incisive comments have often clarified for me the central issues and led to fertile investigations. More than that, the imagination and enthusiasm he brings to analytical thought exemplify the fact that philosophy is a human activity, the practice of which is enriched by a variety of virtues.

I have also benefited from the helpful comments of Bernard Berofsky, who initially stimulated my interest in the philosophy of mind, from Richard Kuhns, and from several discussions with Akeel Bilgrami. In psychology, Julian Hochberg's provocative research and comments have influenced my view of the relation of imagery to perception. I am especially grateful to Dan Lloyd for many years of intellectual stimulation and friendship. The evolution of our mutual interests has been a consistent source of pleasure and motivation.

Much of the work of revising was done during two years as a member of the Society of Fellows in the Humanities at Columbia University. I acknowledge with gratitude the support of the Society. The very congenial and energetic atmosphere there—due largely to the director, Loretta Nassar, and the constant interaction with colleagues and friends—provided a great stimulus to work and made it a pleasure. All of the fellows are due thanks, particularly Richard Andrews, Mary Campbell, and Dilwyn Knox, who made many provocative and useful comments.

The book was completed with support from a research grant from Washington University, for which I am grateful. The research efforts of David Beisecker, who was my undergraduate research assistant during that time, helped bring the project to completion; and the unstintingly cheerful skill and diligence of Jean Kirby made it a tangible reality.

Finally, I would like to thank Cynthia Richards, who read several sections of the book and whose critical acuity helped make the material much more accessible than it would otherwise have been.

The View from Descartes's Window

*If I chance to look out of a window onto men
passing in the street, I do not fail to say, on seeing
them, that I see men . . . and yet, what do I see
from this window, other than hats and cloaks,
which can cover ghosts or dummies who
move only by springs?*
RENÉ DESCARTES

In the *Meditations,* Descartes entertains a well-known fantasy, more prophetic than he could possibly have foreseen, about the reality that might lie hidden behind the scene appearing in his window.[1] It is ironic that the man who said that "the mind must be turned away from the workings of the imagination" should concoct such a fantasy; but then, from his fertile mind sprang the thought that the whole world might be an illusion, created by an evil genius. More ironic still, however, is the fact that one of the most forceful critics of Cartesian dualism, Gilbert Ryle, has accused the father of modern philosophy of promulgating precisely that myth, the reality of which he so seemed to fear. According to Ryle, the Cartesian compromise consisted in making persons into both ghosts *and* dummies, indeed, into dummies inhabited by the ghosts in an impossible interaction of immaterial mind and physical body. But it is sometimes forgotten that Ryle objected just as much to the way in which, on Descartes's analysis, the dummy inhabits the ghost, at least as a model for how the mind operates.

In proposing the substantiality of the mind, Descartes commits himself to what Ryle called a "para-mechanical hypothesis," a pulleys and levers kind of account, according to which "minds are things, but different sorts of things[;] . . . mental processes are causes and effects, but different sorts of causes and effects. . . . The repudiators of mechanism represented minds," Ryle continues, "as extra centres of causal processes, rather like machines but also considerably different from them."[2] Therein lay, as Ryle calls it, a category mistake. Minds are machinelike, on Descartes's model, and not only because they have causal powers. Mental activity is also paramechanistic in the sense that it employs, in the exercise of those powers, *rules* and *representations* of a certain sort: ideas, the relations among which can be regimented along the lines of mathematics. In that case, the relevant principles could be applied systematically to derive results more or less automatically. Thus, what Descartes imagined he saw from his window, a possible illusion he wished to dispel by the force of reason, was, from Ryle's perspective, through that very method deemed to be true.[3]

In recent years, the revival of interest in neocartesian epistemology has at times been associated with a model of the mind that has gone Descartes one better in making what might be called the new paramechanical shift: The computational model of the mind as a thinking machine is no longer a metaphor, according to sophisticated scientific theory. The mind is not like a computer—it is one.

The "computational compromise," as it might be termed, has gone one up on that of Descartes by exorcizing the ghost and endowing the dummy with intelligence. But what makes it still a compromise of sorts is that, in the interest of developing a true science of the mind, it aims to retain a radical distinction between both the properties and the mode of explanation that are characteristic of the program that now inhabits the machine and those that are characteristic of the actual machine itself. In that case, the problem of interaction remains, but in a different guise. The new problem of interaction is not simply locating the computer's pineal gland and then activating the computational counterparts to animal spirits to serve as the vehicle of psychophysical transaction. Rather, it is to make good the claim that there is a form of scientific theory in which the autonomy of thought as a logical process is preserved, while attributing the occurrence of that thought to a physical process governed by laws apparently of a very different sort from those governing thought itself. And that is a problem of theory construction.

The recent insistence that the computational model of the mind must be taken literally is unmistakably a call to arms. For some, the prospect is exciting, the opening of a new scientific frontier. As Zenon Pylyshyn puts it: "Many feel, as I do, that there may well exist a natural domain corresponding roughly to what has been called 'cognition.' . . . The domain of cognitive science may be something like 'knowing things,' or as George Miller colorfully dubbed it, the 'informavores.' . . . Humans and other members of the natural kind 'informavore' [do] precisely what computers do, [and thus] my proposal amounts to a claim that cognition is a type of computation."[4] Yet for others the consequence of adopting this theory, for psychology as much as for society, will be dismal. Indeed, recent expressions of concern have taken on apocalyptic dimensions. As one critic argues, for example: "There is a crisis in contemporary psychology similar in severity and importance to the one that led to the appearance of behaviorism, and . . . [mental] imagery once again plays a central role in the crisis. . . . Unless solutions are found to the problems associated with imagery, there will again be a change in the definition of psychology . . . [and] the effects will be negative."[5]

The reference to mental imagery here is not coincidental. In the past few years, a debate has arisen among cognitive psychologists about whether—or in what form—images might play a role in cognition; and, as these remarks suggest, the matter has become a kind of crucible for defining cognitive science *as* a science. It is the matter in this crucible I want to examine.

To begin, we should note what is being concocted, as older concerns about images melt away and new ones begin to take shape. The current debate owes its particular character to the central place of representational theories of mind in contemporary cognitive psychology. Roughly speaking, a representational theory aims to explain the intelligent behavior of a system in terms of the content of symbol-like states that can be attributed to the system. The crucial question, then, is whether or not those states must be construed to be wholly internal to the system and, if so, how they can be understood to have content. The internality of symbol states, according to most accounts, is essentially the internality of a computer program; thus efforts to show that mental states have content assume that computational and representational approaches to psychology are compatible.

There are, of course, a variety of views on how that compatibility is possible or why it is not; and it will be important later to identify a number of them. For present purposes, however, it suffices to note that all are concerned with isolating the properties of mental states by virtue of which they are the vehicle for cognition. The topic of mental imagery resonates naturally with that concern. The issues lately associated with imagery illustrate larger problems about the nature of mental representation. They thus provide a focal point for the study of the mind and test the plausibility of various accounts of its workings.

There are, at present, two competing views of imagery. Neither denies the existence of mental images or the meaningfulness of the term *image*; rather, both attempt to account for recent experiments, the results of which strongly suggest that imaging occurs in conjunction with certain tasks involving memory and perceptual recognition. One view, pictorialism, as it has come to be called, holds that mental displays are employed in some cases of cognition. Thus an adequate representational psychology must provide an account of the role of images in that sense. The other view, descriptionalism, argues that all cognition requires a linguistic format: All thought is essentially propositional. According to this theory, "imaging" can be understood as a special case of proposition-based computation.[6]

I will argue that neither of these alternatives is satisfactory. Descriptionalism will prove to be false: There are no good reasons to deny a genuinely cognitive function to mental displays, and indeed a strong case can be made that the effective performance of some tasks actually requires them. However, pictorialism is, at present, so seriously underdeveloped that it can claim almost no purchase on the philosophy of mind. Apart from articulating a set of basic procedures that are defined over spatial configurations, pictorialists have not probed the representational properties of displays or depictions sufficiently to produce a fully developed theory.

In part, that lack may be due to the fact that the implications of developing such a theory would be profound. Serious and important arguments have been set forth to show that the very idea of mental pictorial representation or, more broadly, nonpropositional representation, embodies a deep confusion. Further, some critics say, a theory that tries to accommodate nonpropositional representation will run afoul of the canons of good science. The norm here for conceptual coherence and scientific rigor is set by the computational model that now permeates cognitive psychology. I will argue, however, that there are independent reasons for wanting a psychological account of the capacity to visualize; therefore, we must re-examine some of the standards that are assumed to rest at the very foundations of cognitive science.

The basic precept of my account is that cognition must comprise a richer set of resources than the prevailing computational model would allow. However, I should make clear at the outset that, unlike some critics of artificial intelligence research, my intention is not to repudiate that model entirely. Indeed, in order to give an account of how mental resources are exploited, it will be necessary to modify and adopt certain important features of the model. In particular, I will assume, as a method of analysis, that cognition requires a medium with a formal syntax of some kind, which provides it with a logical structure appropriate for the implementation of rule-governed procedures. How semantics come into play is a matter of debate; but, minimally, the account of syntax must be given in terms of the capacity for properties, like truth and reference, on which representation depends. This tripartite framework— syntax, semantics, process—is the starting point from which to begin to define a cognitive function for images.

It will be something of a striking discovery to find good candidates for each of these three features of a representational theory of imagery. The candidates come from the literature on perceptual categorization, picture perception, and what might be generally termed "aesthetic psychology." One virtue of a study of mental imagery is that it provides the opportunity to comprehend systematically research on a variety of fronts that have so far only been nominally related. To be sure, prototypes, mental models, frames, and parallel processes have been treated by certain critics as being of a piece with mental images that depict information: The considerations that militate against images are also thought to undermine claims about the cognitive role of certain related phenomena. Understanding something of the relation among them, however, will serve to reinforce those claims and lay the groundwork for a theory of non-propositional representation.

It is nonetheless crucial to avoid the conclusion that the result of this analysis is simply another sort of language. Pictures and other types of display have properties that make them very different from descriptions in the form of sentences. Without that difference, there would be little point to the detailed explication of the notion of imagery. One way to put the point, although this is by no means the whole story, is to say that operations on images are *analog* in nature, and thus they are in certain respects fundamentally different from digital processes. The payoff for insisting that images are both similar to and different from linguistic representation will thus come at the level of metatheory, for the kind of explanation that many philosophers of science and mind hold to be appropriate to analog processes is supposed to be very different from the kind appropriate to digital processes. While some efforts have been made to show that there is a continuum of representational types, there have been almost no corollary efforts to show continuity among types of scientific explanation. To the contrary, generalizations about a whole class of models have been made, based largely upon the imagery debate, about how those models violate essential conditions on explanation in a fully computational psychology.

I take the position that image experiments confirm the theory that mental depiction plays a role in cognition that is different than that of mental description. This position cuts two ways. To identify the role of mental images, we must see them in the context of computation and rule-governed representation. However, to distinguish mental depiction from description we must enlarge the concept of representation considerably and argue for a composite science of the mind in which there are diverse strategies of explanation.

The analysis of mental imagery will thus constitute a perspective on cognition that has been broadened in three senses: It focuses on imagery and related phenomena, which have been taken for the most part to lie on the periphery of cognition; it argues for the importance of what I have termed "aesthetic psychology" for cognitive science, important particularly to the imagery debate, from which it has been almost wholly excluded; and it aims to circumscribe representation in a way that does not place biological and environmental factors beyond its bound, as has often been the case with recent cognitivist perspectives.

The view from Descartes's window can thus be brightened considerably by seeing just where we stand in relation to our newfound mechanical friends: The computational model gone literal is an effective strategy for progress in cognitive psychology, in that it tests the limits of what is now viewed as the science of the mind. The products of this new paramechanical shift are, in effect, Descartes's grandchildren. What I want to show is that the current state of the art scarcely exhausts the possibilities; and while those possibilities may be accommodated by expanding the notion of computation, the result will be a new theory.

Mental Imagery

CHAPTER ONE

Minding the Brain

The Theory of Internal States

In general, philosophical psychology is concerned with conceptual problems in the explanation of behavior. As a crucial part of that enterprise, it must confront the fact that the most interesting and significant forms of behavior are those that are purposive and intentional; or, to put it somewhat differently, philosophical psychologists must account for the features of behavior we label as purposive and intentional. We assume, for a variety of reasons, that any such account will have to be given in terms of confirmable scientific hypotheses grounded in empirical investigation. However, this is a path along which certain obstacles are strewn. Insofar as the explanation of behavior in causal and wholly materialistic terms introduces mechanism and, along with it, the possibility of determinism, it seems antagonistic to the underlying import of concepts like purpose and intent; that is, it seems to run against the very point of postulating them. But at a more basic level, the problem is that intending to act is inherently goal-directed; thus we are faced with the task of explaining what could be meant by attributing to someone *now* a state that must be specified in terms of the future.

Traditionally, the direction of behavior toward some future state of affairs has been thought to raise the specter of teleology. Teleological explanation is a special type of explanation that "invokes the goal for the sake of which the explicandum occurs."[1] Such an account is at odds with ordinary causal accounts because the terms it invokes are not independently identified. The antecedent condition A of consequent behavior B is identified as a state in which B

will lead to some goal G. Explanation in this sense is said to thwart
further inquiry because it appeals to something like an inherent
tendency toward a goal, and it implies that a basic level of explanation has been reached. That is, as Charles Taylor has put it, "the
fact that a tendency towards a given condition results in this condition neither requires nor admits of further explanation."[2] For
these reasons, teleology is held to be objectionable.

The concept of mental representation provides a partial solution.
In brief, treating purposive behavior as the result of mental representation allows the terms of the explanation to be factored apart.
We need not, nor can we, say simply that directed behavior is that
which is adequate to realize some goal. What is required in addition
is that the agent in question perceives his behavior as likely to
produce the result he wants. And that is to say that his behavior
must be attributed to his mental representation of that result. The
goal in terms of which the behavior is explained is the object of his
action by virtue of the content of the mental states accompanying
the behavior. Thus, goal direction is describable in terms of the
objects of mental states, and ascribing content to the representation
of goals will be a necessary condition, at least, for purposive behavior. Further, the representational properties of the mental states
themselves do not have to be identified by reference to the relevant
goals.

How then are they identified? In what does mental representation
consist? There is no single, easy answer to this question, but the
debate over the cognitive status of mental imagery turns on it, and
so an answer must be given. To that end, I begin with a look at
recent history, in the context of which the question makes sense.
A guiding concern, though not a decisive one, is the fact that we do
represent future and present states of affairs in our use of language.
And linguistic representations share with certain mental states an
important feature: intentionality. That is, they have "reference to
a content, a direction upon an object."[3] We say, for example, "I
want, desire, prefer . . . that p," or "I believe, hope, fear . . . that q."
This suggests that a necessary condition for a theory of representation is to explicate the notion of intentional content. For mental
representation more specifically, the problem is to account for the
attribution of states that are identified in terms of their content to
a physical system like the brain.

To this problem, the computer holds the key. Since we often
attribute intentional states to computers in describing their behav-

ior as goal-directed (when they are said to "want" more information, for example), and since they are so clearly physical devices explicable in causal, nonteleological terms, we have every reason to think that a materialist theory of intelligent behavior can be derived from the computer model. It is important to note, however, that the computer has not always been courted with the same degree of ardor with which it is now embraced, at least by some of its suitors. Indeed, competing theories of cognition can be distinguished by the distance they stand in relation to it.

The philosophy of mind that has been, for many years, the favored view in the cognitive science community is functionalism. Although there are, in fact, various forms of functionalism, many philosophers, psychologists, and computer scientists have shared the general belief that a physicalist account of mental states can be given by identifying those states with functions performed by the brain. To a large degree, the origin of functionalism in its modern form corresponds to early appeals to the computer analogy intended to determine the general nature of mental states. Twenty years ago, for example, Hilary Putnam (who has now changed his view) argued that the problem of self-knowledge, or first-person psychological ascriptions, and the problem of other minds, or third-person psychological ascriptions, could be shown to arise for machines as much as for mortals.[4] The point was not to predict philosophical angst for future computers but to establish a line of comparison that works both ways: If the behavior of some machines can be analyzed in terms of the same kind of psychological states and hypothetical parameters as those characteristic of humans, then, in certain respects, machines will be like humans. If that can be established, it lends weight to the claim that, in certain related respects, humans are like machines. "The strength of the analogy between human behavior and computer behavior," Daniel Dennett declared, "is thus a critical point."[5]

The point, even at the most general level of comparison, is a philosophically substantive one. Since it is clear that the same function can be performed by many different kinds of mechanism, a strong argument can be made that functional state types cannot be identical to physical state types: If functionalism is true, then the identity theory must be false. Some mental states, at least, are functionally equivalent to the states that occur as elements in a computational process. Given the implausibility of classifying brains and computer hardware together as physical kinds, physical type-identity conditions on mental states are essentially out of the question.

This is a point to which I will return shortly, when it will become necessary to blunt it somewhat in order to argue against the radical autonomy of psychology, an autonomy which has its roots in the sharp distinction between function and physical structure. But first it is essential to say more about the notion of a "function." Merely noting a general similarity between mental states and computer functions does not commit one to any theory of the precise nature of the functions in question. In particular, it does not entail realism about mental representation. Indeed, functionalism in its most basic sense is often *contrasted* with representational theories of the mind, for precisely that reason.[6] However, while the character of the kind of states relevant to those theories *is* very different in principle from basic, nonsymbolic, causal relations in terms of which functions may be specified, they are functional states nonetheless. Thus, the mantle of independence that a psychology of mental functions is supposed to wear can come in a variety of styles, depending on the kind of functions with which it adorns itself.

The earliest strategy was to overcome the problem of the intentional character of psychological language by establishing what Dennett has called a *rapprochement* between the mental and physical modes of discourse.[7] This was to be done by ascribing meaning or content to states of the central nervous system, in the sense that the occurrence of covert, internal physical events would be taken as the condition for ascribing mental states to an agent. Given the assumption that the internal events could be identified as physical structures with causal powers, that would constitute a kind of extensional "reduction" of the intentional psychological predicates. Taken only so far, however, the analysis leaves open the question of the precise nature of the functional states.

While there is no doubt, on this approach, that the functions performed by physical processes literally occur, the question remains as to whether those functions should themselves be described in representational terms. Central states may actually constitute an internal representational medium in some sense; but attributing content to them may be construed, instead, as merely a heuristic strategy, based upon their causal connection to overt language use.

A number of critical considerations that bear directly on the imagery debate can be traced back to various points in the evolution of competing theories of intentionality. Indeed, it is important to note that, in certain respects, the problem of rapprochement tends to beg the question against anything like a pictorialist theory of mental imagery. The problem has been set as one of giving a coherent materialist account of the intentionality of mental states, by showing how the intentional language of psychology applies to physical systems. But it is not at all clear, at first blush, that occurrent visual images have intentional content. Therefore, it is unclear how these proposed solutions are supposed to apply to them. This bias, which occurs even in theories that are antagonistic to any realist account of mental representation, will become all too apparent in later chapters. It is illuminating to see where it got its start.

In order to determine the nature of mental functions to which content is somehow to be ascribed, it is essential, of course, to define the concept of a function. While at least six different uses of the term *function* have been identified in the literature, the core theory[8] holds that functional states are like the logical states of a computer in the following respect: A logical state is given by a description of the internal state considered in abstraction from its physical properties. The state is essentially an element in a set of conditions in terms of which, along with a specification of input, output can be specified.

The assumption that the inputs and outputs of these internal states must be specified in *symbolic* terms moves the account considerably closer to a representational theory. It amounts to the adoption of the Turing machine as a model of the mind. As Hilary Putnam has noted, "anything capable of going through a succession of states in time can be a Turing machine," but the machine is itself largely an abstraction, "essentially a computational procedure for problem-solving . . . [which is], in principle, physically realizable."[9] To that extent, it is described by a machine table that specifies state transitions in terms of input, output, and mathematical transformations.

One criticism voiced early and often reiterated, however, was that advocates of this model tend to conflate two very different kinds of mental phenomena. On the one hand are *occurrent states*—passing thoughts and images, for example—that initially seem to fit well the analogy to the logical states of a computer. On the other hand are more or less enduring *features*, such as beliefs and preferences, that do not seem fit in any obvious sense. Insofar as the theory is a theory of occurrent states, it has no bearing on mental features, which simply do not occur.[10]

The criticism is very important with regard to assessing the representational status of mental states. A central assumption of much of cognitive psychology is that intelligent behavior is the product, not simply of the occurrence of strings of symbols, but of relations among beliefs, desires, and other propositional attitudes. It is in terms of these relations that we define the rationality of behavior. In what, then, do the Turing machine's beliefs consist?

A general, initial response is this: The conditions for mental features "should be given by reference to some *abstract* property of the organization of machine tables," themselves.[11] In other words, beliefs and desires have their counterparts in the *computational* states of the machine rather than in any individual logical state through which it may pass in realizing the program that gives it the particular computational character it has. That character constitutes the tacit knowledge, rather than the explicit representation of information, that gives the system its computational power.

Once again, however, a question can be raised about how literally this analysis should be taken. As a merely schematic analogy, it amounts to an account of propositional attitudes in terms of a theoretical set of relations among functional states. Just as the states themselves can be described as literally symbol-like or not, so too can the beliefs defined over them be construed as representational states with a capacity for content or not. The identification of mental states in terms that derive their meaning from their role in some sort of theoretical network is a general strategy compatible with several very different kinds of theory.[12] To define the essential character of a mental state in terms of its relations to other states does not amount to much until the nature of the relations is specified.

In the next section I will set forth reasons for favoring a realist construal of both mental symbols and propositional attitudes; and in later sections I will argue that a convincing case against beliefs has not yet been made. There is in that position a curious irony. To a large extent, the obsession with propositional attitude psychology has weighed heavily against pictorialism. Although the point has been generally obscured, a very useful way to describe what is at issue in the imagery debate is this: How do nonpropositional images fit into a predominantly propositional attitude psychology? The rather widespread assumption among those cognitive scientists committed to a literal use of a computational model is that they don't. Among those who hold the minority view, little has been said to show how they do. I want not only to show how they do fit in but to argue that their fitting in actually strengthens the commitment to propositional attitudes as well.

THE FORMALITY CONDITION

When the relational model of the mind, according to which mental states are individuated by their place in a network of relations of various sorts, adopts a specifically computational guise, the relata are taken to include representations. In Fodor's words: "Mental states are relations between organisms and internal representations; and causally interrelated mental states succeed one another according to computational principles which apply formally to the representations."[13]

The formal application of those principles depends on the fact that the internal representations have formal features. That is, computational processes apply in virtue of the "shapes of the objects in their domain," and in particular "in virtue of (roughly) the *syntax* of the representations," without any reference to semantic properties like truth and meaning.[14] Symbol tokens can be arranged into complex shapes that exhibit a grammatical structure, and in so doing, exemplify rules of usage as well as construction. Thus, there is said to be a language of thought, inscribed in the brain in the form of neurochemical activity, which functions as if it embodied sentences, or sentencelike formulae. All the power of higher order cognitive processing is given as a bonus, so to speak, for investing in the hypothesis that there are, in effect, word shapes in the brain that have syntactical features.

It is important to keep in mind that the notion of *formality* is used in two senses. One sense is just "to have form," that is, formal features; the other sense is "to be governed by formalizable rules," by virtue of those formal features. This distinction matters because it is the first sense of form that allows the mental symbols to be realized in physical structures, but it is the second sense of form that will distinguish cognitive processes from the physical processes that instantiate them. In brief, while both structures and symbols have formal features that can be correlated or mapped onto each other, only symbols are governed by formalizable rules, like the rules of logic. Thus, the formality condition allows us to have it both ways: Mental representations are instantiated in physical states but are not reducible to them. Thus employed, the computational model does not confuse form in the sense of shape with form in the sense of rule governance, as has sometimes been claimed.[15] Rather, it exploits a relation between them.

A formalist psychology in this sense is taken to have one very important virtue. To cite one example of this view, Georges Rey argues that the computational model of the mind offers the only remotely plausible solution to the mind-body problem. It provides the only viable explanation of how thinking mind arises from un-thinking matter.[16] It is true, of course, that there are causal se-quences of representations that can only be explained by reference to what the representations are about; for example, it is the fact that my thought is about *p* rather than *q* that will lead to a certain behavior. The problem is that what is represented is outside of the representational system and need not be causally connected to it. Thus, as Pylyshyn puts it, "so long as we remain materialists . . . we cannot attribute causal powers to the semantic content of rep-resentations."[17] Rey echoes those sentiments: "By and large," he says, "what's mental is rational, what's rational is syntactic; and what's syntactic is computational and mechanical."[18]

The advantage of syntactic formalism is that it makes possible a systematic psychology where otherwise there would be only a pro-grammatic one. Moreover, it accounts for certain notorious char-acteristics of mental representation. Regarding the systematic character of psychology, the problem which the formalist approach aims to circumvent is that it is not possible to individuate mental states in terms of causal relations between an agent and his envi-ronment. A number of arguments have been given on behalf of this view. For example, Nelson Goodman has made what Fodor calls the epistemological argument, which says that there can be no canon-ical descriptions of the kinds of things that cause behavior: "The object before me is a man, a swarm of atoms, a complex of cells, a fiddler, a fool, and much more. If none of these constitute the object as it is, what else might?"[19] However, it would not follow from this limit on knowledge that a systematic theory of causal relations could never be mounted on any categorical postulates. Fodor is him-self chary of the epistemological base for this argument and offers one stronger in its implications.

Although in principle we can claim to identify types of cause and effect, Fodor argues, we will never be able to give a completely systematic account of stimulus-response conditions. Accurate descriptions of stimuli will depend on the full development of physical theory. Physics is always evolving, so those descriptions will be, to say the least, a long time coming. But this argument is not very compelling either. Provisional definition is endemic to all of science; yet it does not undermine the possibility of theories that are adequate and acceptable in the interim.

In some cases, of course, there may not be ascertainable causal relations that could be used to ascribe content to mental representations, for example, when one thinks about fictional entities or future events. It is possible to try to establish a circuitous causal chain in those cases. For example, the griffin about which I am now thinking may have been constructed from parts of lions and eagles. Alternatively, it may be that beliefs about and images of future events are connected to those events by way of a common cause: The causal chains that lead to both the mental representation and its object will originate in the same conditions.[20] However, it is by no means clear that the content of creative mental fiction can be exhausted by variations on a fixed vocabulary, nor that it has the conjunctive character that this analysis implies. Further, there is a problem with specifying the cause that is common to a belief and its object in a way that does not beg the question. Suppose that I believe falsely that it will rain tomorrow. To try to establish identity conditions for that belief in terms of the antecedent accumulation of clouds that would ordinarily produce rain, but now do not, would be a desperate attempt to save the theory by invoking a single cause that is actual in the case of the belief and only possible in the case of the rain. What these considerations suggest is that, logical possibility aside, the primary problem with causal theories of the mind is that they just do not hold much promise of success.

It is important to note that these arguments against causal theories need not count against all externalist theories of mind. The latter are concerned to establish external conditions on, say, the ascription of a belief; and those are not bound to include establishing a causal chain between the believer and the object of belief. The conditions that make the utterance of a belief true, for example, may impose constraints on when we would assign a particular belief to someone; but that does not entail that the conditions must be construed as the causal antecedents of expressions of the belief in question.

Nonetheless, it remains to be shown that a noncausal externalist theory of the mind can account for the behavioral effects of beliefs. A strong argument on behalf of the formality condition is that those effects must be understood in terms of the form in which a belief occurs. That is, requiring cognitive theories to be couched in terms of a formal medium in which mental representation occurs helps us to understand the fact that we cannot ascribe beliefs to people *solely* in terms of their content. When my young niece tells me she learned in school that Louis XIV was a despot, I cannot attribute to her the belief that the Sun King was a despot, because, for one thing, she may not yet have heard of the Sun King. Propositional attitudes like belief are, in that respect, opaque to the substitution of expressions that have equivalent meanings but that are different in form; and one explanation of that fact is that their occurrence is bound to the particular form in which they are expressed, that being indicative of the form in which they are held.

Thus, the conditions warranting the assertion that "x believes p" will not warrant the assertion that "x believes q," despite the fact that p and q describe the same state of affairs. It is highly unlikely that the difference can be explained by the truth conditions on p and q, that is, as part of a psychological theory.

Despite the appeal to the syntax of linguistic representation as the primary example of formalism, the formality condition should not be taken at the outset in too rarified a sense. As Fodor notes, for example, visual images and operations on them can satisfy a basic formality condition: They have formal features in terms of which they can be individuated.[21] The question is whether they are formal in a sense that is adequate to assign them a cognitive function. What counts as adequate in that respect requires more analysis than has so far been given. The aim here is to establish a basis for describing the psychological reality of mental states, but in a way that is sufficiently general not to prejudice the issue against the image. To that end, we must turn to a consideration of the occurrence of mental forms and the nature of access to them.

THE NATURE OF ACCESS

In what sense can a brain, being the sort of gray matter that it is, be said to instantiate a language? To be sure, we can, in principle, assign languagelike functions to neural processes, warranted, as I have suggested in the preceding section, by an analogy to the computer. But the question remains about how precisely to understand the basic functions out of which a representational capacity arises. In particular, we must clarify how those functions stand in relation to the rules that are part and parcel of linguistic representation. In what respects, we need to know, are such rules effective?

It is important to note at the outset that this problem is not the same as what John Haugeland has called the "mystery of original meaning."[22] The question he raises is this: How can we avoid the conclusion that states of mind, on the computer model, are essentially empty? The challenge of original meaning is to show that content occurs naturally, as it were, in a mind construed to be a formal system; for the content of mental states would not seem to be derived from an interpretation of symbols like the reading of a book. That is indeed a concern to be confronted, but it is a problem with several dimensions. Thus we must first address a more basic matter, one which bears on the larger issue, and that is to make clear the sense in which a formal system actually "employs" rules and representations.

In the standard account, it is manifestly not the case that a system employs rules in the sense that it represents the rules explicitly in any form, say as a list of described moves and positions in the production of mental sentences, against which it then checks its computational activity. That would, of course, lead to an infinite regress, since the model implies that the checking would also have to be checked and the rule representations constructed according to further rules that in turn would have to be represented. Rather, the idea is that the rules are encoded in the system insofar as representations embody canonical form. Sentences, for example, may be well formed in a standardized way that exemplifies rules of construction and, thus, encodes them implicitly. Similarly with computation and inference: Valid argument forms in logic, for example, serve as rules of inference. A system is said to obey rules if its behavior comports with them systematically and consistently over time, and the behavior is caused by properties to which the relevant forms are attributed.

Nonetheless, it is still necessary to ask, wherein lie these canonical forms? It is sometimes said and often assumed that the most natural way to identify these forms is to see them embodied in series of electrical discharges in the brain, which form the basis for a binary code (since they either fire or they do not). However, the mere fact that there may be localized discrete firings itself tells us nothing about the most appropriate way to describe the neural functions in general. As a principle of theory construction, what one wants is to construe neural functioning in a way that does not beg important questions. The problem with laying too heavy an emphasis on the binary character of electrical impulses is that to do so lends a credibility that may prove to be entirely undeserved to three claims: that the code in question is essentially abstract and fully dissociable from the structure that instantiates it; that representational formulae and computational procedures are always deployed in a linear sequence; and that the underlying nature of the formal system is necessarily digital. Taken together, these claims militate strongly against a variety of nonpropositional models of cognition and, in particular, against a pictorialist theory of mental imagery. To avoid introducing this bias at the outset, I want to propose an alternative way of grounding representational functions in neural processes.

One helpful way to understand the formal individuation of mental states is to treat patterns of neural activity as functional patterns as well, that is, as configurations. For example, an updated version of something like Hebb's proposal for perception might provide a model.[23] The first time a baby is exposed to a triangular shape, according to this model, its eye will be drawn naturally to the line forming the edge of the triangle and will move back and forth along the contour. If by chance a corner happens to come into the visual field, the eye will tend to shift direction and follow the line around the corner. This is the pattern of stimulation whenever corners are present. If the baby is repeatedly exposed to this pattern, it will develop a cell assembly, that is, a group of cells in the brain that responds to that particular pattern. For a triangular shape, a set of three such cell assemblies firing in sequence will create what Hebb called a phase sequence. Once these are established, the eye movements required to produce them in the first place are no longer necessary. A glance at the triangle starts the phase sequence firing, as a kind of reverberating circuit in the brain.

This conception of the reality of formal figures in the brain is entirely neutral regarding the nature of the form in question. The functionally defined configurations may be said to have a syntactical form or they may not. The figural approach to the individuation of mental states is, in fact, perfectly consistent with the digitalness of a binary code. To be sure, a series of light flashes, ones and zeroes, dots and dashes, or whatever, need not have a functional shape. Nonetheless, the series can be construed to be an array of sorts, extended in time. There are, as it were, word tokens, the inscription of which depends upon a basic capacity for figural imagery.

Of course the introduction of functional patterns in which rules of composition are potentially embedded in no way implies the need to postulate access through internal scrutiny. The formal individuation of these figures, whether they be discrete notational forms or something else, is a matter of formal interpretation, which proceeds by implementing procedures in which the forms are included. On a machine model, there is internal "computational access" in the sense that the output of one process can become the input of another, which is thus of a higher order.[24] Typical access relations of that sort establish the identity of the states over which the processes are defined. To that extent, one could say, the formal interpretation is made by the system itself. As the cell assembly–phase sequence model illustrates, the point applies to nonlinguistic forms as much as linguistic ones. In that respect, the figural analysis is compatible with general principles of computational access. Indeed, it provides a grounding for them.

The further effect of this analysis, however, is to call attention to a level of functional description below that of the vocabulary and grammar of the language of thought. The purpose of this distinction is twofold, in the elaboration of a theory of mental imagery that aims to locate itself within a larger conception of the nature of cognition.

First, recognizing that there could be a basic level of functional configurations frees the next level up from the fetters that some computational theorists want to impose on it. Specifically, a theory of functional configurations lays the groundwork for an account of the rich resources of the human mind, by permitting the effects of knowledge to penetrate further into mental operations than some propositionally based computational models would admit.

Second, this understanding of the nature of access to the forms by which mental representations are individuated mitigates the tendency toward wholesale antinaturalism. Fodor argued at one point that adopting the formality condition is tantamount to embracing "methodological solipsism."[25] More recently, Stephen Stich has argued similarly for a principle of autonomy, according to which the focus of cognitive science should be exclusively on mental syntax.[26] The argument is that formal individuation of mental states is not

only necessary but sufficient for the explanation of intelligent behavior. Other representational theorists (including Fodor himself in
later writings) deny this and hold that an account of the attribution
of content to mental states is a necessary part of representational
theory. This, of course, is a major issue, to be addressed in later
chapters. Merely articulating a notion of internal access relations,
as I have done here, by itself does nothing to resolve that question.
However, it lays the groundwork for understanding how images, in
their own way, can be said to have content. Since the social context
of sophisticated beings is a highly structured ecological niche, we
can better understand how the mind integrates with its environment if we begin with an understanding of the prelinguistic base
out of which intelligent behavior arises. There is then at least a real
sense of biological continuity that runs from mentality to motility
and maintenance in the world.

Thus I will argue for a certain understanding of mental representation. In essence, the logic of the argument as it has been set forth
so far can be summarized as follows: A theory of mental representation is required to account for intelligent behavior. Such representations must be in a broad sense functional states of physical
systems, for no other account meets the requirements of psychological theory. Representations function by virtue of formal features, since it is only by means of such features that content
attribution within the system is possible. The formal features need
not be taken to result from a mechanism that is fundamentally
digital; rather, the features may be understood to be functional configurations. An account of the individuation of mental representations in that sense is essentially equivalent to attributing an
imaging function to neural processes. This function will be basic:
It is presupposed by mental representation in any form, whether
sentential or pictorial; thus, it is a condition for cognitive theory.

It remains to be shown that form for an image can be represen-
tationally relevant in some further sense bearing on the current
debate. It is essential to consider first a set of arguments that go
right to the heart of the matter regarding the larger significance of
this debate. Any fully developed theory must satisfy a more detailed
set of methodological constraints than have so far been considered,
if it is to establish its scientific credentials. We must confront the
question of what counts as a good theory in this domain.

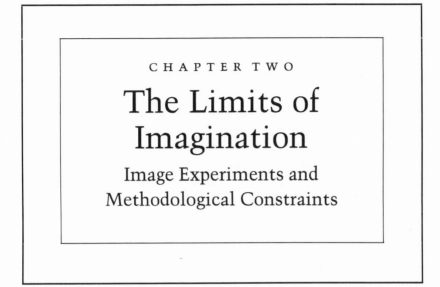

CHAPTER TWO

The Limits of Imagination

Image Experiments and Methodological Constraints

"Imagination is more important than knowledge," Einstein is supposed to have said. In what sense might that be true? In part, of
course, the statement recognizes the value of ingenuity in constructing new scientific theories; but since Einstein's own brand of
scientific genius is known to have been stimulated, on one important occasion, by his reflecting on a mental image of himself chasing
a ray of light, perhaps we can take his declaration somewhat more
literally. That is, perhaps we can understand him to be saying that
human intelligence cannot be defined just in terms of theoretical
knowledge. It also requires, as so many psychologists past and present have claimed, an explanation of the capacity for concrete visualization: of past experience, of future goals, of solutions to problems. In short, it requires an account of the capacity for mental
imagery.

But what are the limits of imagination in that sense? In putting
it that way, I am really asking two questions. Exactly what purposes
are mental images supposed to serve, especially according to current
cognitive theory? How can an empirically grounded, logically rigorous theory of mental imagery be given? Or to put the second
question somewhat more polemically: Can a psychological theory

that includes mental images satisfy accepted canons for good science? The two questions are the focus of this chapter.

It is easy to see, intuitively at least, why it might be not only helpful but even essential to make use of a mental image of some kind in performing certain cognitive tasks. "*That,*" I think to myself, "is a beguiling face," recalling last night's chance encounter with a mysterious stranger. In what does my thought consist? On the surface, it appears to require a visualized image to which the demonstrative term *that* can refer. Otherwise, the thought is incomplete; and I will never be able to find that stranger again.

It is true, of course, that I might have, instead of an image, merely a list of features, which I run through in thinking of that face: those deep-set eyes, that dark straight hair, the little rose tattoo upon the left cheek. Yet clearly there will be problems with substituting a list for the image. Suppose that tonight when I go to the club for a rendezvous, I discover two people who happen to be wearing identical rose tattoos. So I retrieve my list. But after all, a list only goes so far, and, as it happens, each of these two strangers matches this one item for item. *No* list will ever be exhaustive. There must be another way.

One other way has been suggested lately by the research of Roger Shepard and his colleagues, and by Stephen Kosslyn, among others. Any theory of mental imagery that aspires to a philosophical perspective on cognitive psychology must take account of these fascinating experiments that have, in fact, sparked considerable controversy. But it is important to note that this controversy has two parts, one part substantive, the other methodological. On the face of it, there is an overt disagreement between pictorialists and descriptionalists about how to interpret the empirical data. To be precise, the question is whether both theories do, in fact, adequately account for all the results of these studies, and, if so, how?

However, some psychologists have argued, this is a debate that may be impossible to decide empirically.[1] Certain arguments mounted recently within the debate recognize this difficulty and, in effect, move to higher ground. From that perspective, they naturally invoke a higher authority, indeed, the authority of what passes for canon law in science, namely, what is sometimes called "metatheory." On that basis, they argue not that one or another theory is incompatible with the empirical results but rather that some types of theory are just methodologically unsound. Those theories would thus be eliminated on a priori grounds.

It is therefore necessary to address the methodological issues first. After a stage-setting discussion of the experiments in question and the two primary accounts of them, I want to consider in some detail certain analyses that would effectively determine what the nature of mental imagery would have to be as a construct in a bona fide scientific theory. Aside from the logical priority of these analyses, a large part of their interest derives from the fact that they bear upon so many aspects of recent psychology. Zenon Pylyshyn, in particular, claims that his objections to Kosslyn's theory of mental imagery can be applied to perceptual prototypes, mental models, frame theory, and parallel distributed processing.[2] This suggests how the mental imagery debate is not nearly so parochial as it might seem.

It also suggests that the distinction between method and substance is, from the philosophical perspective, somewhat artificial. This is, of course, true in the sense that metatheoretical concerns are philosophically substantive; indeed, they are the stuff of philosophy of science. However, I will argue that the distinction is also artificial in the sense that, in the case of mental image studies, the invocation of those purportedly antecedent conditions on theory construction actually *presuppose* a particular theory. Of course, this will not come as a shock, but it will call attention to the fact that arguments about methodology in cognitive science are arguments with a history. Some of that history was traced in the preceding chapter. I want to pursue it somewhat further here, to show how it corresponds to the evolution of a theory. It is in this theory that the details of the computational model of the mind have been worked out. The point will be to show that a pictorialist account can satisfy the requisite constraints on cognitive theory, and, in showing how that is so, to begin to argue for a view of the further evolution of it.

The argument for mental pictures must proceed by increments. It must be shown, first, that a psychological theory that incorporates them is possible in principle. For the sake of analysis, I have divided the task in two. What follows will focus on the methodological part. In the ensuing chapter, the more explicitly substantive issues are addressed; and I will argue there that none of them should be decided against mental pictures either. The larger challenge then remains: to give a positive account of imagery in cognition.

THE IMAGE CONTROVERSY

Although questions about the role of images have been a recurrent, stalwart issue in psychology, until those questions were reformulated recently, images have held only antiquarian interest for the analytic philosophy of mind. This reformulation was prompted initially by a series of ingenious experiments conducted by R. N. Shepard and his associates. These experiments seemed to show that subjects performed operations upon visual images in carrying out certain tasks.[3] The most notorious experiment demonstrates what might be called the "rotation effect." Subjects were shown sets of drawings constructed according to three different rules. The subject's task with each pair of drawings, which appeared on a screen while the subject's head was kept still, was to indicate whether or not they were the "same," that is, could be rotated so as to coincide. As it turned out, subjects responded with a 95 per cent accuracy rate; but the important data had to do not with accuracy but with reaction time (see figures 1 and 2).

The subjects reported that they were rotating mental images in order to answer the experimenter's questions, and the data appear to bear them out. If mental rotation really occurred, the larger the rotation required, the longer it should take to decide whether the drawings are the same or different. The statistical evidence clearly shows that reaction time was a function of the deviation of the image from its original orientation. Thus the hypothesis was confirmed.

A second type of experiment showed similar results, in this case giving evidence for what can be called the "scanning phenomenon." In 1973 and in later experiments, S. M. Kosslyn and others argued that if mental images are spatial in nature, then they should be capable of preserving relative distances between the parts of the objects that they represent.[4] In one experiment, people first learned to draw a map with a mythical island that contained seven objects (for example, a hut, a tree, a rock). These objects were located so that each of the twenty-one inter-object distances was at least ½ cm. longer than the next shortest one. After learning to draw the map (that is, having memorized it in some sense), subjects were asked to form an image of it and to focus mentally on a given location (each location being used as a focal point equally often). On being presented with a word (sometimes naming an object on the island, sometimes not), subjects were asked to locate the object and,

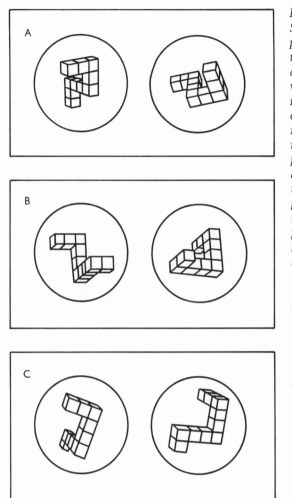

Figure 1.
Subjects looked at pairs of perspective drawings and had to say whether they were rotations of each other. The A pair is a rotation on the plane of the page; the B pair is a rotation in the third dimension, perpendicular to the page; the C pair cannot be made to match by any rotation. From Roger Brown and Richard Herrnstein, "Icons and Images," in Imagery, *ed. Ned Block. Copyright © 1981, the MIT Press. Reprinted with permission of the MIT Press.*

when they had found it (if they could find it), to push a button. In theory, the longer the distance from the focal point, the more time required to respond, assuming that scanning was involved. This, too, was confirmed (see figure 3).

These results have been taken to support the attempt to provide a functional account of mental imagery in terms of pictorial representation. One obvious advantage of pictorial representation would appear to be the ease with which it conveys information integrated

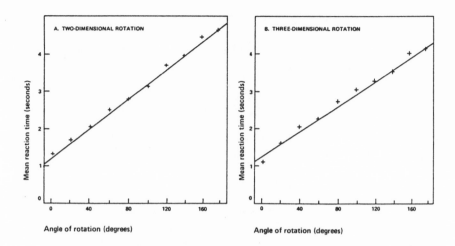

Figure 2. The time to respond to pairs of stimuli as a function of the difference in degrees between the members of a pair. The left graph is for A in fig. 1; the right graph, for B. From Roger Brown and Richard Herrnstein, "Icons and Images," in Imagery, *ed. Ned Block. Copyright © 1981, the MIT Press. Reprinted with permission of the MIT Press.*

into a unified whole. Its merit is simplicity and directness. To represent a scene verbally will require either a potentially infinite set of sentences or inferences from a selected set. To represent a scene pictorially, however, requires but a single picture, albeit a complex one; and the information it contains implicitly may be discovered in the representation without involving derivation in the sense of logical inference.

There is, of course, an important philosophical precedent for describing mental representation in terms of images. The idea that the mind is a representational system is roughly the view that cognition consists in performing operations on mental symbols of some sort. This theory is nothing new. It is, in fact, part and parcel of eighteenth-century British empiricism, in which imagery played a fundamental role. According to that school of thought, ideas, often in the form of images, are combined according to certain principles of association, notably, resemblance. But, aside from the problem of locating these representations in a mental space, a part of their conceptual inadequacy is due to the fact that resemblance is a notoriously insufficient basis for an account of representation. "After

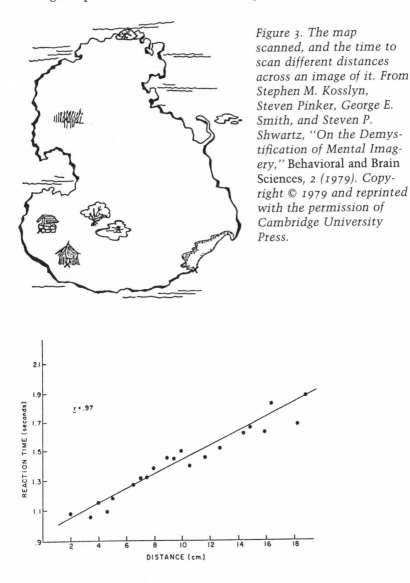

Figure 3. The map scanned, and the time to scan different distances across an image of it. From Stephen M. Kosslyn, Steven Pinker, George E. Smith, and Steven P. Shwartz, "On the Demystification of Mental Imagery," Behavioral and Brain Sciences, 2 *(1979). Copyright © 1979 and reprinted with the permission of Cambridge University Press.*

all," Plato noted, "everything resembles everything else up to a point."[5] Furthermore, as Goodman has pointed out, resemblance is a symmetrical relation and picturing is not. If *A* resembles *B*, then *B* resembles *A*. There is nothing in resemblance alone that allows us to say that *A* is a representation of *B* or that *B* is a representation of *A*.[6] For these and other reasons, pictorialists claim that the real theoretical explanation of isomorphism lies in the abstract properties of the protomodel.

Insofar as images are construed as pictorial displays in a spatial medium, their identities as pictures are intended to be purely functional. That is, a mental "picture" might be defined by the numbered coordinates of locations, the distances between which can be determined by mathematical calculation; or it might be defined by a matrix in which spatial relations are represented by activated cell adjacencies, as in the case of a cathode ray tube or television screen. Even in the latter case, however, an image is an *iconic* representation of an object, not by sharing perceptible properties with it, but by being formed and transformed according to laws that can be correlated with laws that are operative in the world of tables and chairs. In that world, for example, the time of an object's movement is a function of the distance covered and speed. The mind would represent this property pictorially if the time it takes to imagine that movement can also be shown to be a function of some lawlike relation between mental representations of distance and speed.

Specifically, what it means to say that there are mental pictures is that the physiological properties of the brain function like physical magnitudes to represent spatial relations among objects in the world by virtue of what some writers have called a "second-order [that is, functional] isomorphism."[7] Because I think that term is too general, I prefer to say that the representational relation is one of "nomic similarity." That is, second-order, emergent properties of applying physical laws to external world events will be replicated in second-order, emergent properties of applying biological principles or causal generalizations to brain events. So, to use the same example again, speed, time, and distance relations will be preserved in patterns of neural discharge identified by hypothesis through psychophysical measurement or some other kind of test.

In essence, this means that operations on images will be defined as modes of analog processing in one sense of the term. Imaging is defined by a relation between physical values assigned to a spatial medium and physical values assigned to an object or event in just the way that, for example, a mercury thermometer represents temperature or a pressure gauge represents pressure, namely, by correlating column height or pointer angle with kinetic energy or molecular activity.

Consider, for example, the scanning phenomenon.[8] There is a physical law governing the perceptual scanning of a real map, that is, time equals distance divided by speed, $T = D/S$. It is possible that this law could be correlated with the process of image scanning if, say, D = electrical potential between two points and S = current flow, and the relation between these can be translated into another governing the amount of time it takes to transform images.

It is the conception of second-order isomorphism, or as I have called it, nomic similarity, that protects the thesis against the charge that it would require a homunculus in residence, whose job it would be to perceive the image on the screen of a mental cathode ray tube, a metaphor sometimes employed to explicate the theory.[9] Nonetheless, the concept of a functional array is one that has provoked a skeptical reaction: "One should, however, be cautious in what one assumes to be an intrinsic function that is *instantiated* by the underlying biological structure, as opposed to one that is *computed* from tacit knowledge by the application of rules to symbolically represented beliefs, goals, and so on."[10]

The central objection to the array model is that, although it is feasible to correlate brain events with world events through corresponding laws defined by mathematical relations, the attempt to explain mental representation in this way is mistaken, because the relevant relations are *semantic ones.* That is, the purported isomorphism of image to object, according to this argument, is not simply unproven but is implausible. The reason is that the character of imagery—for example, the time it takes to imagine an object's movements—depends upon prior knowledge, and this tacit influence of knowledge and belief upon imagery implies that the functional properties relevant to the definition of images are semantic capacity and the ability to play a role in quasi-inferential cognitive processes. That is, in experiments, differential reaction times are said to show that physical laws governing the time of various external spatial operations apply by correspondence to different internal transformations of a certain type. But the observable differences might just as well be due to the fact that subjects were asked to perform mental tasks of different types and some utilized more tacit knowledge than others in performing similar tasks.

For example, in one study subjects were shown trick photographs of tilted pitchers containing fluids whose surface orientations were artificially set as inappropriate angles relative to the horizontal.[11] Half the subjects tested could not recognize the anomalies in the photographs. Postexperiment interviews revealed that every subject who recognized all such anomalies could articulate the principle of fluid invariance in some form, whereas no subject who made errors could give evidence of understanding this principle.

According to descriptionalism, this study shows that it is not necessary to postulate mental pictures or other nondiscursive images to account for these differential reaction times, because the observed differences might just as well be due to the fact that subjects were tacitly exploiting knowledge about the perceived rotation of images rather than actually performing the rotation. And that knowledge is propositional, stored in a sentential format, not a pictorial one.

It is important to note that the mental task will vary depending upon the extent to which one is required to incorporate past perceptions into one's imagery. It is one thing to imagine the eruption of Mount St. Helens, another to imagine seeing the eruption. In that case, it could simply be that in the image experiments varying complexity means that some computations using mental descriptions take longer than others; but it is more likely that the experimental situation is such that subjects naturally take their task to be to imagine engaging in the process of rotation or scanning itself, and in doing so, they simply replicate the known characteristics of those processes. That is, the argument goes, subjects do not form an image and then scan or rotate it. Instead, they spend time imagining *that* they are scanning or rotating it, indeed, just about as much time as they believe the corresponding physical operation would take.

There is no doubt, of course, that these experiments do show the effects of knowledge upon the subjects' behavior: Response times differ from one task to the next because of what the subjects know about the spatial relations among the cubes or map locations they have just seen. But the crux of the matter is that many people claim not just that those effects could be explained in terms of computations using mental sentences, but that they must be.[12] As I have suggested previously, a useful way to express the reason for that claim is this: Knowledge is a function of belief; thus, the utilization of knowledge must be defined in terms of logical relations among beliefs and other propositional attitudes. And, as far as we know, the propositions that provide the content of those beliefs can only be expressed in the form of sentences. It is this claim—that nondiscursive images are inappropriate for an account of intelligent behavior because they do not fit comfortably with belief-desire psychology—that makes the matter of more than parochial interest to those of us who enjoy a pictorially rich dream and fantasy life.

To evaluate the force of the argument against pictorialism, we must pursue it in greater detail. Precisely why nonpropositional

images should be excluded from a rigorous proposition-based computational psychology—or, if admitted, how their role is restricted
—is not clear simply from the fact that an alternate account is
available. However, the primary focal problem for pictorialism,
raised by the tacit knowledge argument in its strongest form, is that
the theory lacks an adequate analysis of the notion of nonpropositional representation. Without such analysis, the contribution of
visual images to cognition will not be understood.

THE METHODOLOGICAL ARGUMENT

One important characteristic of pictures is that "parts" of pictures
correspond to "parts" of objects represented. The systematic, lawlike correspondence between image and object consists in the fact
that, besides the representation of the object by the image as a
whole, some properties of the image represent properties of the object. It is this fact that supports a range of inferences and counter-
factuals.[13] For example, I can see from the picture of a tiger that
tigers have stripes, whereas I can at best infer that from the word
tiger, based upon learned associations. Second, pictures are marked
by a *continuity* of representational content; and this, it is argued,
derives from a more basic feature, namely, that there are intrinsic
lawful relations holding among physical properties. There is a systematic, lawlike correspondence between image and object, in part,
because properties of the image represent properties of the object;
and it is by virtue of this fact that the image as a whole represents
the whole object (taken as an object of representation, not in and of
itself). Whatever else pictures are, one way to understand their part-
whole, continuous nature is derived from their analog character.

The notion of an analog process is a rather ambiguous one; but
as I have noted, Shepard's research assumes that it refers to a relation between physical values assigned to a spatial medium and
physical values assigned to an object or event external to that medium. Analog processes thus exploit physical properties—say, the
adjacency of one point to another in an array of electrical impulses—to represent the spatial features of objects in the world. But,
according to critics like Pylyshyn and Haugeland, it is precisely in
that respect that analog processes are too intimately bound to the
physical properties or structure of the medium. Their exploitation
of physical properties in this way makes them noncognitive, vir-

tually by definition. The similarity of laws by which an image represents its object, these critics say, is manifestly not an abstract, logical, inferential relation, to which the rules of cognition can apply. As it turns out, the formal features of images are not formal in the right way; that is, they are law governed rather than rule governed. Therefore, such analog processes should not be employed in the explanation of genuinely cognitive behavior.

In an important sense, this position extends a long-standing claim in the philosophy of mind about functionalism referred to earlier, namely, that descriptions of mental functions cannot be reduced to descriptions of biological or physical functions. This is so not just because they often employ terms that make no explicit reference to physical properties and because many different kinds of physical structure or biological process can perform the same function in different machines or organisms. In addition, complete reduction, were it possible, would vitiate psychology because physical or biological laws will miss the right level of generalization relevant to the explanation of behavior.

The fact that cognitive processes involve the manipulation of symbols means that the physical structure and the cognitive process are supposed to be governed by very different kinds of "laws": the laws of physics or biology, on the one hand, and the laws of logic or practical reason, on the other. The former are laws in the sense of being nomological generalizations, that is, regularities, often expressed as equations, on the basis of which predictions can be made. The latter, on the other hand, are laws in the sense of being rules of inference that express relations of logical entailment or confirmation. These are determined by the forms of arguments and abstract relations among terms employed, not by causal relations among physical properties. The outcome of any process governed by such rules cannot be predicted on the basis of a specification, however complete, of antecedent physical conditions and a general law. As Haugeland puts it: *"Particles* have neither choice nor difficulty in 'obeying' physics—it happens infallibly and automatically. People, on the other hand, often have to work to be reasonable; following the rules of reason is hardly infallible and can be very difficult. But this means that there cannot be an explanatory dynamics of thought, which is at all comparable to physical dynamic theories; the respective rules and laws in the two cases are deeply different."[14]

So, for example, we might say that cognition is necessarily "stimulus bound" by way of perception; that is, basic sensory mechanisms must be responsive to physical properties as inputs. Yet there is nonetheless considerable latitude in how such stimuli are categorized and interpreted and, thus, considerable latitude in the kinds of cognitive operations that are dependent upon them. In a certain respect, it is precisely that flexibility that is taken as a hallmark of intelligent behavior; and it happens to be a characteristic of the computational model that many philosophers and psychologists adopt.

Haugeland has developed this line of analysis in detail in his critique of the foundations of cognitive science.[15] He distinguishes three kinds of explanation. Roughly, the first is at the level of physical description of the system; and it is a variant of the sort of deductive-nomological explanation appropriate to classical mechanics. Haugeland calls it "derivational-nomological" because the explanation consists in deriving mathematically one sort of equation from another, such as Newton's derivations of Kepler's laws.

The second type of explanation, which Haugeland calls "morphological," is at the level of functional-causal description. It is directed at a functional capacity of some kind, appealing to the form or structure by virtue of which the system has the capacity in question. One often finds such explanations in biological science. For example, DNA replication is explained in terms of the ability of a double helix—two strands of uniquely matched sites—to separate and link up with an exactly similar new one.

The third kind of explanation is labeled "systematic." What makes it systematic is that the explanation is given in terms of organized cooperative interaction in a system made up of distinct parts. The emphasis here falls on the interaction. That is, while something like the DNA model does involve distinct functional components that contribute to an overall ability, Haugeland argues that they work only by a kind of "orderly summation" rather than by interdependent cooperation involving a variety of roles. In that respect, the DNA model differs from the explanation of how, for example, a radio or an engine works.

The importance of the distinction between morphological and systematic explanation for images becomes clear when picturelike representations are contrasted with linguistic ones. The latter involve an "intentionally interpreted articulated typology" that provides the components on which a systematic explanation depends. Pictures do not have any obvious, specifiable set of elements that are systematically interdependent. Thus, though Haugeland does not put it exactly like this, interactions among nondiscursive images will not be explicable systematically, but only, at best, in terms of their morphology. In effect, Haugeland makes the previously noted differences between pictures and descriptions into differences in modes of relevant scientific explanation, thus drawing out the larger implications of the debate.[16]

Pylyshyn makes a similar point. Cognitive processes are "nomologically arbitrary." That is, transitions from one computational state to another can involve arbitrarily many causal laws, since many different physical states can instantiate a given computational state; therefore they "cannot be explained the way natural events typically are explained in science."[17] Nonpropositional images, however, are components in analog processes; as such, they are supposed to be bound to the medium in such a way as to make them *not* nomologically arbitrary, virtually by definition. Because analog processes are identified by values assigned to physical properties, they can be explained by causal laws applied at a certain level of functional description. In that respect, according to this argument, they must be noncognitive.

Pylyshyn thus concentrates on one rather central aspect of analog processes, their employment of physical properties. As he notes, it is possible to give a theory of the logical or quasi-linguistic properties of an analog system. Goodman argues that a system is analog if it is both syntactically and semantically "dense," that is, if it provides for an infinite number of ordered characters in the form of utterances, inscriptions, marks, and so forth, and of ordered compliance classes or denotata, so that between each two there is a third.[18] More simply, in analog systems there is a mathematical continuity among representations or representations of intermediate states. However, Pylyshyn argues, although several such characteristics are attributed to analog systems ("everything from mathematical continuity of representations to the simple requirement that the representations go through intermediate states"), all derive from the feature that there are intrinsic lawful relations among physical properties.[19] The pictorial format contains implicit relations that manifest themselves in emergent properties comparable, for example, to the "rigidity" or "contour" of objects. The fact that pictures contain more implicit information than descriptions is related to the feature of continuity, which is characteristic of analog processes. Insofar as mathematical continuity and the representation of intermediate states are connected and derive from (or reflect) the intrinsic lawful relations holding among physical properties, it is those relations that allow the compositional exploitation of whole-object representation to have representation of parts of the object by parts of the picture.

Pylyshyn therefore concludes that continuity, intrinsicness, naturalism, holism, and so on are not really the issue. The problem for pictures as modes of mental representation is that their function is "instantiated or exhibited" rather than computed. Thus operations on any such images would occur at a level below that at which systematic explanation in cognitive terms is employed. They would belong to the level of basic functional components.

Human behavior is thus theoretically complex in that it calls for different kinds of scientific explanation, and confusing these explanatory modes is supposed to have pernicious consequences. This claim is not simply a warning against wide-eyed mentalism, which sees intelligence in the automatic door opener and desire in the rhododendron as it turns toward the sun. Nor is it a scientific manifesto against a mechanistic and deterministic account of behavior. The pernicious effects against which the methodological conditions protect are explanatory failures; and the confusion that produces them can be both subtle and compelling.

As an argument for the need for a special form of explanation to account for behavior involving cognition, these points do have force. To cite a well-worn example, it is not simply a description of physical inputs—say a ringing bell, the smell of smoke, or my neighbor's yelling "fire"—that will explain my running out of the house. It is rather what these things represent to me by way of the content of the belief that they all produce, together with a characteristic desire to avoid getting burned. However, as an argument for a fundamental dichotomy between types of explanation in all cases, these points are not persuasive. This is so for several reasons.

First, it would be a confusion of a classic sort to conclude that, since our concept of a function is different from our concept of a physical structure, we must not specify any function in terms of any physical properties.[20] Although there are principled differences in the kinds of scientific explanation I have discussed, it does not follow from that difference in principle that the kinds of *property* in terms of which the explanations are given must be fundamentally different. Thus, even if analog processes are to be understood in terms of numerical values assigned to physical or biological events, and in that respect are susceptible to explanation in terms of physical and biological laws, it cannot be said that they must therefore be excluded entirely from generalizations about intelligent behavior, at least on that ground alone.

Second, nomological flexibility in cognition and the norm of rationality against which it is judged are important; but one must be careful not to misunderstand the nature of that importance. These features manifestly do not give intelligent beings the kind of autonomy that would ignite a gleam in the libertarian eye. As rational and flexible as they might be, cognitive processes are not causally undetermined. Rather, they are flexible in the sense of being abstract and hence performable in different ways. Further, they are capable of improving through experience and are often guided by heuristic strategies for weighting various possible ways of achieving a goal. But what reasons have we for thinking that these are characteristics that demarcate cognition in such a way as to exclude nonpropositional images? Indeed, since they are often treated as heuristic aids, analog operations utilizing such images might be said to *enhance* cognitive flexibility and intelligence. Although they may not be on a par with the power of a mental language, would it not be possible to treat analog operations using images as genuinely cognitive in certain respects and, in particular, allow that they affect and are affected by knowledge and beliefs? Surely images in that sense could at least be components in processes for which systematic explanation is appropriate. Imagery could be said to play a role in cognition simply because whenever images are given an interpretation by being brought under a description, they are then essentially implicated in systematic explanations of cognitive behavior. That is, explanation of that sort will necessarily depend in those cases upon the analog properties of images.

In *The Language of Thought*, for example, Jerry Fodor describes one kind of thought that seems to be logically incomplete without some kind of mental display to accompany it.[21] Suppose I think to myself, "I'm looking for a man who looks like that." The argument is that the demonstrative term *that* requires a picture or illustration to which to refer; otherwise, the sentence will not be well formed. Even if it is only heuristic, here is a case in which a nondiscursive image makes a contribution to the performance of a cognitive task. Thus, one could argue, insofar as the sentence-image complex is used in some kind of logical inference or practical syllogism, leading to other sentence-image complexes, mental pictures and the like just are included in cognitive processes.

Unfortunately, there are two major problems with this argument for a pluralistic cognitive psychology. First, Pylyshyn has argued that, even if images under descriptions were to serve as a medium for cognition, that role would itself be, strictly speaking, noncognitive. Since his argument is methodological, I want to pursue it further here. But, second, even if all metatheoretical objections can be surmounted, as I will argue they can, there will still be a problem of explaining how it is that images come to *be* components in cognitive processes, that is, in what their relation to mental sentences consists. In effect, mental images fall between the cracks of scientific explanation. They are neither simply physical structures nor full-blown, rule-governed representations. They appear to be formal configurations without formal rules. To the extent that such is the case, it is not easy to see precisely how they should fit into a symbol system, as a point of logical analysis. That is the topic of the next chapter. First we must consider a powerful argument that serious antecedent constraints must be imposed on the theory, regardless of the precise nature of sentence-image fit, which will keep the image from playing any real cognitive role.

COGNITIVE PENETRABILITY

Historically, the importance of Alan Turing and his famous machine lies largely in the fact that they gave us an initial model for the functional description of neural activity. Such a model is of value because it guides theory development by eliminating potentially irrelevant features and restricting the theory to a certain vocabulary of description. The methodological point of the Turing machine analogy is that it supplies the normal form for a functional account of psychological types. However, the viability of this model has been called into question lately, in part because the normal form it supplies for cognitive theory is not restrictive enough. It simply does not impose sufficient conditions on theory construction to satisfy important metatheoretical concerns that would allow psychology to develop in ways that would enhance its scientific stature. And as we revise those conditions, some cognitive theorists have argued, mental images must fall by the wayside.

In part, the model that Turing gave us for the functional description of mental representation derives its legitimacy from a well-known test that he devised. According to the Turing test, any machine smart enough to fool an interlocutor into thinking it has intelligence does, indeed, have it; but that is not enough to establish the relevance of a computer model for human cognition. It is not enough because of the problem of simulation. Merely simulating intelligent behavior can mask the fact that the actual operations underlying the behavior are very different from those that we humans employ. In order to avoid that problem, we must be able to say what counts, not just as the same behavior given the same input, but what counts as the same behavior produced *in the same way* or *by the same process*. In that respect, the challenge to cognitivism is clear: If we are going to postulate internal states as causes of behavior, we need something more than a mere machine analogy to identify particular kinds of mental states or processes and to justify the attribution of them to the human mind.

There are in fact two related problems here. One is to distinguish genuinely *cognitive* processes from physical or biological ones; the other is to identify different *types* of cognitive process. Each of these has its own special danger. In the first case, the danger lies in unnecessary mentalization of what are really complex physical events. In the second case, the problem is somewhat more subtle. It is not simply that the wrong cognitive process might be postulated in the face of behavioral data, though that of course is a central concern. Rather, the danger lies in allowing a certain looseness in the concept of cognition itself, in the specification of the distinctive features of a cognitive process type. It seems natural to want to relativize, at least to some degree, the identification of higher-order cognitive processes to the nature of the task at hand. As a result, it may be thought that certain fundamental operations on which cognition depends in some cases actually constitute it in others. That is, what is merely the means for implementing higher-order mentation for one purpose itself becomes, for other purposes, the higher-order end that is implemented by operations that are more basic still. But, one might argue, there must be some principles that constrain theoretical relativity of that sort. Otherwise, one could too easily succumb to the temptation to construct a relatively open-ended theory of cognition that can be doctored up as new data keep coming in.

In *Computation and Cognition*, Pylyshyn has developed what he calls the "cognitive penetrability" condition.[22] He argues that in order to distinguish one type of cognitive process from another, we need some measure of the complexity of the processes in question. According to one measure, two processes are the same if they use the same resources (for example, time or memory capacity) in response to the same inputs. Whether or not that would actually be sufficient to differentiate and evaluate processes, what is significant about a measure of this sort is that it assumes that there are primitive operations—encoding information, storing the information in memory, and the like—and that these primitive operations are fixed for all tasks. The mental resources that they are typically required to use will have to be constant. Such primitive operations, along with the basic terms over which they are defined, are part of what has been termed the "functional architecture" of the system.

Pylyshyn argues that a fundamental tenet of theory construction in cognitive science is that the functional architecture must be assumed to be utterly stable. In particular, it cannot be *cognitively penetrable,* that is, responsive to the influence of knowledge and belief. Permitting changes in the foundations of thought of that sort is said to undermine the basis for defining process equivalence and thus to weaken the theoretical value of the account as an explanation. If the very medium of thought is allowed to change under the influence of belief and goal fixation, then it can no longer be construed as the medium for belief and goal fixation, except in the most ad hoc and unprincipled way. If the calculator's capacity to perform arithmetical operations can be changed by the repeated storage in its memory function of remainders, sums, and products, then the principled distinction between representation and causation is supposed to break down, and the whole computational model is thought to lose its explanatory force.

Applied to the imagery debate, the argument then is this: The rotating and scanning of figures postulated by pictorialism are basic operations. Their function is "instantiated or exhibited" rather than symbolically computed by the operation of rules on representations: "They can thus be viewed as characteristics of functional architecture."[23] Functional architecture is cognitively impenetrable. However, Shepard and others have shown that the process that underlies the behavior associated with "imagery" is cognitively penetrable. Therefore, mental imagery must actually consist in computational relations defined over descriptions.

As I will point out shortly, Pylyshyn's argument here is two-sided: Problems with pictorialism are cited to demonstrate the need for his methodological constraints, which are in turn used against it. There is nothing particularly inappropriate in that, given the intimate link between methodology and substantive theory, and in light of the fact that he gives independent grounds for his views on both. However, in the end I want to argue that he begs the issue against pictorialism in another way. To lay the ground for that case and to see what is at issue, I consider first some objections to the cognitive penetrability condition in general.

A number of reasons have been cited by commentators for doubting the value of, and the need for, the cognitive penetrability condition. These points are important, but I think that the critical responses to Pylyshyn have sometimes overlooked the real force of his argument. That force lies in the implication that the state of the art in cognitive theorizing *requires* the kind of conditions he would impose: No accounts that dispense with such conditions can be adequate, he thinks. As Fodor has said in a different context, "The history of science reveals that when a successful theory comes into conflict with a methodological scruple, it is generally the scruple that gives way."[24] What Pylyshyn denies, in effect, is that there is yet any theory that conflicts with his scruple that can succeed. To attack the scruple leaves unanswered the challenge to show signs of success, a challenge to which his conditions are inherently linked.

It is true, as some critics have charged, that confusion results from taking the cognitive penetrability condition to solve both problems in the identification of cognitive processes noted earlier. That is, the cognitive penetrability condition is used in two ways: within the organism, as a condition for something being a part of the computational subsystem; and within that computational subsystem, as a condition for not being a part of the functional architecture. But apart from ambiguity, the problem is that there are grounds to think that both noncognitive biological processes and basic operations at the level of functional architecture can show the effects of knowledge. Thus those effects do not serve to demarcate the realm of higher-order cognition.

On the first count, as a solution to the problem of isolating the computational subsystem as a whole, Pylyshyn's condition would appear to fall before counterexamples. Digestion and pulse rate, for instance, are affected by the knowledge that an object of strong desire or fear is close at hand.[25] And on the second count, as a means of segregating cognitive processes per se from more basic operations, the standard is subverted by the relativity of the distinction between higher and lower functions. There is no single level of abstraction at which *the* functional architecture is located. For example, while a rule of inference may serve the ends of diverse proof procedures, there are still more basic principles on which it will itself depend. It would therefore be a mistake, critics have said, to assume that architecture is fixed across cognitive tasks, in the sense that operations at that level never vary under the influence of acquired knowledge.[26]

However, it could be replied that both of these arguments are beside the point. Of course, one might say, there can be many co-incidental cognitive effects in the physical system; but Pylyshyn warns us appropriately to make some theoretical provision for the fact that they are not effects of the right sort. Or, to put it differently, the cited examples are merely the effects of knowledge; they do not constitute the employment of it. Though my heartbeat is affected by the particular content of my heart's desire, and its pounding may produce the thought, "be still my heart," those causal relations do not map onto inferential relations. And that is because the pounding is not a sufficiently complex process to count as the locus of representational form or content. Its relative simplicity makes it a natural candidate for the category of noncognitive process, given that such a distinction is essential to a viable computational model.

Similarly, to merely state the theory-relativity of a functional architecture description is to overlook the fact that the central objection to permitting change in the functional architecture is a *metatheoretical* one: Any account that allows such changes will have to describe the behavior of the system with variable degrees of abstractness. The objection is that the theory will be too ad hoc, since it will permit great latitude in identifying the variables needed to account for the behavior in question. Thus, Pylyshyn can be taken to be arguing generally as follows: Unless a comprehensive account of types of cognitive tasks and corresponding level changes is given, the cognitive penetrability condition is required. In a comprehensive account, permitting level changes would not be an ad hoc device. But there is no such account, so a methodological constraint must be imposed.

Once it becomes clear, however, that Pylyshyn's concern is to *regiment* theory construction in accounting for changes in the system at various levels, then a new set of objections can be made. The point of these objections is not that the cognitive penetrability condition is too artificial and not mandated by the facts of the matter. Rather, it is that, as a device, the constraint has its own inherent weaknesses; and, in any case, it is born out of a norm for good science that is entirely too single-minded.

So, for example, one could argue that it is actually descriptionalism that lacks sufficient theoretical control. Pylyshyn says that tacit knowledge "could obviously depend on *anything* the subject might tacitly know or believe concerning what usually happens in the corresponding perceptual situations" and "the exact domain of knowledge being appealed to can vary from case to case."[27] In that respect, one can argue, the theory is virtually unfalsifiable: Some sort of tacit knowledge could always be postulated to account for results.

Moreover, as Steven Pinker argues, the ad hoc character of a theory is a relative notion.[28] It may favor one theory over another but generally cannot be used against a single theory. One should not criticize a theory for having the requisite number of degrees of freedom, based on the way the world is. From the computational point of view, Pinker argues, a good theory is one that produces correct behavior in simulation testing and handles the most data. And that, he argues, is exactly what array theories of imagery do. Such theories provide for more facts in a more satisfactory way than alternative accounts do. Thus, for Pinker, the availability of pictorialist accounts of imagery research undercuts rather than supports the need for Pylyshyn's constraint.

There is, in that respect, a special challenge that remains for a theory of imagery, and that is to explain the sense in which processes that depend on the pictorial or displaylike properties of images are cognitive. For Pylyshyn, the development of cognitive abilities is not itself cognitive. Thus any change in the basic constituents of cognition through learning would be, at best, only conducive to the performance of higher-order processes. That conclusion makes clear how tendentious and stipulative the cognitive penetrability condition is in general. But it also shows how operations like image rotation and scanning, if they are not to be taken as intrinsically simple or especially basic, need to be defined more precisely in terms of their particular contribution to something like truth preservation or content relations. For, in an important sense, it is the coherent relations among such semantic properties that make mental representation theoretically manageable.

Here the two sides of Pylyshyn's argument become apparent. His pessimism about the viability of pictorialism, and hence the invocation of metatheory, derives from his version of the argument, noted earlier, that nonlinguistic images lack an adequate formal structure to enter into productive formal relations. For Pylyshyn, nondiscursive displays are never more than foundational units, because they essentially function like simple terms. They lack grammatical structure. As a result, they do not participate in any external syntactical relations with other images. What this means is that any changes in such images cannot be explained in terms of semantic properties, for which syntax is a vehicle. Therefore, they are especially inappropriate constructs to locate at the level of cognition. Lacking the capacity to express true and meaningful propositions, nonlinguistic images in analog processes really are, as Kosslyn calls them in the title of one of his books, ghosts in the mind's machine. They are forbidden from haunting the realm of cognition because we cannot say of them, as we plausibly can of changes in linguistic terms through learning and perception, that they *make sense.* That is, we have no real theory of ways in which images might serve the ends of intelligence or otherwise contribute to the cogency of one's mental life.[29]

It is, of course, fairly easy to cite counterexamples to the argument that there are no genuinely higher-order pictorial processes. While single images and simple routines may not show the effects of knowledge and belief, and hence may be only basic components in cognition, there is no reason to think that a series of images and a concatenation of spatial routines will not show those effects. If so, then they may be flexible and not deterministic, hence susceptible to systematic explanation in principle. For example, in motion pictures in which a scene unfolds by way of spatial projections from one frame to the next, the relations among the frames serve to define the perceptual identities of the objects represented. It is simply a fact that there can be more and less effective ways to represent a scene pictorially (by choosing, say, between panning and tracking), and the choice of a procedure can clearly show the effects of acquired knowledge.

But it is one thing to cite counterexamples and another to give an alternative account to accommodate those counterexamples. And in the absence of such an account, it will always remain open to the computational conservative to make the one argument that is the hardest to answer and that bares most blatantly the deepest commitments of much current cognitive science.

That argument is this: Suppose that these examples are genuine cognitive processes, but ones that cannot be reduced to an account in purely linguistic terms. Nonetheless, the fact is that ultimately they must be describable as employing representations that can serve as the objects of belief and desire, that is, propositional attitudes, the relations among which constitute the coherence or incoherence of our mental life. Whatever their special characteristics, the pictures and relations among pictures I have mentioned must be shown to be appropriate to serve as the object of such attitudes, analogous at least to the constituents of propositionally expressive sentences that ordinarily play that role. And that is a way of asking for something substantial, namely, a theory of the means by which pictures can be understood to play a role in the attribution of *content* to *thought*. The examples I have mentioned suggest that they do play such a role; the question is how.[30]

Let me then summarize what I think can be concluded from all of this. At bottom, I have argued for two points. One is that the appeal to metatheory, which represents an admirable struggle for scientific credibility and disciplinary definition, has been somewhat abused in connection with mental image debate. But the other point is that mental image research has lent itself to this attack by what might fairly be called narrow-mindedness, that is, by not considering sufficiently the concept of representation it employs and by focusing, naturally enough, on rudimentary operations.

In general I would argue that the need for a methodological standard for identifying cognitive process cannot be met by isolating *in advance* the components of the process that show the effects of knowledge and belief. Rather, it requires a conception of the ends the process is to serve and the rule-following competence required to reach those ends. The requisite properties of the medium follow from that; they do not determine either the ends or the rules. The cognitive penetrability condition is the product of a prior commitment to a computational model of a certain sort, one which is fundamentally propositional in nature. Thus, as a methodological constraint, it begs the question against pictorialist theories of mental imagery. That is so not simply because it is an expression of a particular computational model but because it is invoked on the assumption that no other analysis of imagery of sufficient depth and rigor can be given.

Some have argued that a theory of cognition in which the burden of explanation falls largely upon logical relations among mental sentences will probably fail to account for the creative insight required in mathematics, philosophy, and the sciences, as well as for the ability to grasp the overall sense of a theory. It would follow, interestingly enough, that an exclusively propositional or sentential theory would be unlikely to provide the conditions for its own generation. Whether or not that is so, the methodological conditions set forth in connection with certain theories of that sort seem to cast a pall over cognitive psychology. Of course, the evolution of the standards by which we evaluate admissible theory types is always going to be retarded, to some degree, by the fact that it has to conform to rules sanctioned by whatever theories are presently available. But some visions of science, in this respect, can be more productive than others. Maybe that's what Einstein had in mind.

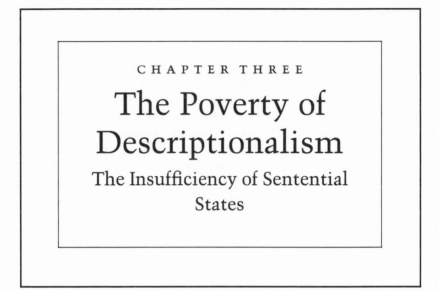

CHAPTER THREE

The Poverty of Descriptionalism

The Insufficiency of Sentential States

In "The Man Who Mistook His Wife for a Hat," Oliver Sacks recounts the tale of a man, Dr. P., who, due to neurological damage of some sort, had lost the ability to recognize perceptual objects in the normal way, even very familiar ones like his own brother's face. "Ach, Paul!" he said when shown a portrait of his brother. "That square jaw, those big teeth—I would know Paul anywhere." But, one might ask, was it Paul he saw, or just his features, on the basis of which he made a reasonable guess? In Sacks's words, Dr. P. "approached these faces . . . as if they were abstract puzzles or tests. . . . Thus there was formal, but no trace of personal gnosis. . . . The visualization of faces and scenes—this was profoundly impaired, almost absent. But the visualization of schemata was preserved, perhaps enhanced."[1]

Of this fact, contemporary cognitive theory can give no account; for, according to the theory, we all should see the world pretty much as Dr. P. does, and we do not. That is, computational psychology would explain all perception as an inferential process of the sort of which Dr. P. was capable. Yet his lack of perceptual content is pathological. Ordinarily, we do not make the kind of mistakes that were characteristic of this unfortunate but admirable man. For his part, Sacks draws an interesting parallel: "By a sort of comic and

awful analogy, our current cognitive neurology and psychology resemble nothing so much as poor Dr. P. . . . Our cognitive sciences
are themselves suffering from an agnosia essentially similar to Dr.
P.'s. . . . [He] may therefore serve as a warning and a parable—of
what happens to a science which eschews the judgmental, the particular, the personal, and becomes entirely abstract and computational."[2]

That is right. However, Sacks disregards a philosophical problem
that has plagued attempts to produce an alternate vision of cognitive
science. His own vision is detectable in the description of what the
current state of the art leaves out: the judgmental, the particular,
and the personal. But that description glosses over a fundamental
difficulty. It is virtually a commonplace of the philosophy of mind
and knowledge that the judgmental and the particular are, in certain
respects, essentially different. To be sure, they can be conjoined, in
the sense that thinking depends, at some point, upon seeing and
hearing. And cognitive psychology does, indeed, purport to account
for that. Like Sacks, I think it has failed; but I want to propose both
reasons and a remedy for the failure.

In part, the admirable efforts of cognitive scientists to enhance
the credibility of their discipline by laying a solid methodological
foundation for it are born out of a concern to avoid theories that
are not well developed and precise enough to be put to the test. For
some critics, pictorialism is such a theory. But the charge of incom-
pleteness and imprecision has, at times, been turned against them.
Kosslyn, for example, offers a rebuttal of Pylyshyn in this way: "In
fact, Pylyshyn has presented some general metaprinciples for a theory, not a theory itself. . . . The tacit knowledge accounts may represent the ultimate in unspecified theories."[3]

The point is, no doubt, overstated. In what follows, I will outline
certain details of how descriptionalism aims to account for imagery
as a species of computation. Nonetheless, it is quite true that the
application of that account to some important dimensions of mental
life does remain undeveloped. There are reasons to think that no
development will be forthcoming. In considering these aspects, all
of which are cognitive in a legitimate sense, I want to argue that a
theory of mental representation specified wholly in terms of sentencelike states cannot account for them. It will then remain to
give an analysis of how such states can occur together with visual
images in the performance of cognitive tasks.

In its computational guise, strong sentialism holds that, apart from restrictions on symbol vocabulary, all formal operations utilized by the system are, in effect, assimilated to operations by virtue of syntactical structure. As an instance of this type of theory, descriptionalism treats imagery in particular as a sub-mode characterized, for example, by ease of access, a lack of quantifiers, inclusion of irrelevant data, and certain kinds of primitive operations.[4]

The format, in this case, is said to consist in a "Fregean configuration," that is, in a relation between function signs and argument signs, the structure of which need not correspond to the structure of what it may denote. By definition, it requires explicit notation of the relations or operators distinct from the representation of arguments. In this format, internal representations consist in "structured descriptions," which differ from linguistic descriptions in that they cannot be externalized as sentences. This is so because the symbols involved may not have corresponding lexical labels in any natural language and because the descriptive structures need not be scanned in a fixed sequence, as is the case with sentences.

Nonetheless, the use of the term *description* in this context is taken to connote the following: (1) the representation must be constructed out of a vocabulary of available concepts; (2) it has a capacity for reference and does not represent by resembling its object; (3) it has a semantics defined by a nonperceptual interpretation function; and (4) it captures psychological complexity in terms of "symbolic" relations, not by geometry or physical arrangements.[5]

Analyzing how we employ these descriptions, Pylyshyn says, "We are presumably interested in finding a psychologically adequate form of representation as well as a logically adequate one. In particular, we are interested in accounting for certain properties of natural intelligence." In the case of imagery, "the single most intriguing property of imagery, and the property that appears ... to distinguish it from other forms of deliberate rational thought, is that it has a certain intrinsic autonomy," in terms of required represented properties (for example, shape and size), susceptibility to unconscious control, and consequent link to creativity.[6]

The belief that syntactic subroutines will account for such features so far amounts to an article of faith. Other critics of the proposition-based computational model that lies behind descriptionalism have argued that there are grounds for doubting whether this faith will be rewarded. They have focused on the capacity for insight and perspective as a kind of creative ability, arguing that it is a capacity for which a proposition-based model is ill suited. And they have linked that capacity with other important phenomena, notably in certain perceptual and memory tasks, in the exercise of skills, and in the psychology of emotion and mood, which, for independent reasons, are also not captured by the model. The argument then is made that nonpropositional images and related structures can be used to give a more adequate account of these matters. With that general conclusion, I agree. But the problem is that we do not fully understand how such images function and, in particular, how the phenomena in question are related. It will be useful, therefore, to consider some of the problems associated with insight, visual reference, skills, emotions, and moods as part of the larger argument for an integrated theory of cognition.

VISUAL REFERENCE AND DETERMINATE QUALITIES

A helpful starting point is given by the observation, noted earlier, that sometimes a picture or display is required to complement a thought in sentence form to give the thought a determinate reference. Thomas Natsoulas has argued that a "degree of perceptual determinateness is often required by intelligent behavior, a degree that cannot be provided in most cases by the conceptual aspect of a perception. In such cases, it is by virtue of the *qualitative presence* of the object or scene (to be behaved towards) that the respective mental episode's reference is fixed."[7] Since the same can be said for some representations drawn from memory, it is important to determine precisely in what this qualitative presence consists and how it might contribute to the fixing of reference.

There are, I suggest, actually *two* ways in which percepts and images might be said to provide a qualitative presence. One is by constituting an experience of a certain sort; the other is by representing perceptible properties in a visual display. It is important to distinguish these ways in order to understand how images function. Neither of them can be said actually to fix the reference of a particular thought. However, images as representations are essential, in some cases, to establish the *capacity* for reference. And, understood in a certain way, the qualitative character of imagery facilitates a cognitive role for emotion. I want to consider briefly the two modes of qualitative presence, as a preliminary to separate treatments of these larger topics on which they bear.

It might be thought that images in perception and memory are like *qualia*, at least in some respects. Qualia are states with a particular qualitative character (as distinct from informational content) which can vary by degree and intensity. Sensory states, like pain, and pure color experiences, like seeing red, are qualia of the classic sort. As mental pictures, one could expect images to provide some phenomenal properties of just this kind. At a minimum, they exhibit primary qualities like shape and size, if not secondary ones like color. Further, even images limited to primary qualities have properties that can vary by degree and intensity: vividness, luminosity, contrast, resolution, and so on. Perhaps it is in these respects that they constitute a qualitative presence.

There is, however, a fundamental difference between images and qualia. Mental images in the form of pictures or other displays are not qualia of the classic sort, since they are taken to *represent* perceptual qualities, as properties of their objects, rather than to constitute a qualitative experience. Of course, images will have their own properties, but those need not be the same as the perceptual qualities of their objects. A picture of a square, blue box need not itself be square or blue. The blue squareness is, instead, a part of its content.

"Felt qualities," on the other hand, do not have content in this intentional sense. Pains and pure color sensations are not representations of pains and colors; indeed, they are not about anything at all. Although of course they will have causes, there is no need to try to define relations among qualia in such a way as to allow them to be mapped onto the world wherein their causes lie. That there is no need for, and no possibility of, such a mapping is suggested by a number of considerations. Hardly anyone would think that we require either a classification of the causes of pain states or a theory of the appropriateness of their occurrence under some conditions and not others. Qualia, in contrast to thoughts and beliefs, are not conditioned in this way. We do not ask for the justification of a pain state or color experience; nor do we try to elaborate appropriateness conditions for them, which would be somehow analogous to truth conditions on belief. They just do not have the kind of internal structure and, hence, content that would warrant the effort.[8]

Nonetheless, it is true that the manner in which images are supposed to represent spatial relations is by "preserving" them through replicating some of their properties. To that extent, the distinction between representing and having qualitative features does not show that mental images are entirely without qualitative character. Indeed, in light of the fact that images are components in analog processes, there are reasons to think that they exploit precisely those properties that make experience qualitative.

For example, in response to some notorious arguments that purport to show that functionalism fails to capture qualia,[9] Paul Churchland has suggested that phenomenal properties might be explained in terms of physical processes that happen to instantiate the corresponding sensory function.[10] Thus sensory states will be essentially functional states to which physical composition contributes a qualitative character. Therefore, one might argue that, because images are components in analog processes and analog processes depend upon the assignation of physical values to a spatial medium, images should be understood to function partly the way sensory states do in Churchland's account, and that is, not simply by employing the physical composition of the medium in the generation of primary quality images, but by actually incorporating it into the image.

Expressed in that way, however, the argument would rest on a mistake. The simple but critical point is that the physical values assigned to the spatial medium and the operations that utilize them are, in principle, just as logically independent of that medium as are any other functions. The rotation of a particular shape does, of course, presuppose certain secondary, emergent properties of physical objects (for example, rigidity). But to obtain those properties, it is not necessary to implement the routine in any particular kind of physical structure, except within certain limits. Indeed, the assumed rigidity is just as much a functional property as the shape itself is, or the rotational process. This point is critical for the argument that there can be higher-order routines involving nonpropositional images that exhibit flexibility.

To be sure, images can have qualitative character in the same sense that other functional states do; and, insofar as that character derives from biological processes, images are especially amenable to it. That is so, at least in the sense that they are functional patterns attributed to neurochemical configurations. But images are not *reducible* to qualia in that sense; and I will argue that, while their capacity for felt quality is an important part of their relation to emotion, their effectiveness in that regard is primarily due to pictorial properties.

In any case, it is clear that, if a qualitative presence were provided by images in this sense, it would not serve to determine a reference. Given that two people can see the same shade of red or feel the same piercing, burning sensation under very different kinds of stimulus conditions, while those qualia do provide a determinate qualitative presence, they do *not* determine the actual reference of any corresponding thoughts about what one sees or feels.

A similar conclusion must be drawn about images as modes of mental representation. What they determine is not actual reference, but rather referential capacity. Their contribution is essentially a contribution to the form of a complex mental representation. That is, however, a very important contribution; and to see why, it will be useful to consider how a computational account of perceptual determinateness would look without an imagistic complement.

In an early article in which he is concerned to show the relevance of artificial intelligence research for cognitive psychology, Pylyshyn claims that AI models are empirically constrained because pattern recognition can be construed in terms of "natural kinds" in a certain sense. Rather than responding to a simple physical characterization of patterns, artificial intelligence must recognize classes defined by psychological criteria, "in the sense that they taxonomize the world in a way relevant to capturing psychological regularities."[11] According to Pylyshyn, all physical events are intrinsically ambiguous, in that they are subject to various interpretations. Therefore, psychologically relevant generalizations must be made in terms of internal representations, independently of any specification of their content in causal terms. There are indefinitely many causal chains in terms of which a given thought or propositional attitude might be specified; thus, any interesting psychological generalization will be lost amidst the diversity. This is, in effect, Fodor's argument for an opaque rather than a transparent psychology of behavior.

As an example of how this account would work, imagine a robotic eye in the form of a camera connected via an analog-to-digital converter to a memory.[12] Light impinges upon the photosensitive surface and is ultimately translated into patterns of polarity switches in magnetic cores in the memory. The camera's input can be encoded numerically, and ultimately the patterns of magnetic polarity become symbolic bit-patterns. Thus, symbolic outputs describe physical inputs. The symbolic and the physical overlap.

The significance of the example is that, while the system is connected to the environment for input, the particular source of light creating a given pattern is irrelevant to the formal and functional identity of the internal state it generates. Perceptual form does not derive from patterns of light energy; rather, it depends upon the instantiation of representational types that are supposed to be specified formally, that is, in terms of syntax. Pattern recognition is a rational procedure. To incorporate it within the computational model, Pylyshyn and others have argued, requires that perception be handled indirectly as quasi-linguistic.

Recalling that the dissatisfaction with this model concerned the need for a greater degree of "determinateness" than the model provides in establishing perceptual reference, one can see two possible interpretations of how it fails. One is that perception is more direct than the model allows. The other is that the kind of perceptual categories it employs are inadequate for some tasks. I want to consider them both briefly; the point will be to show that it is only the second problem that nondiscursive imagery helps resolve.

It is clear that the advantage of an account that includes nonpropositional images is not that it can avoid the classic problem of indirect realism in epistemology. The perceptual counterpart to memory images, "percepts" as they have been called, are interpretive structures interposed between sensation and recognition. Thus they are liable to bias by way of the organization of the system. The degree of determinacy that they are supposed to provide in perception and memory cannot be a matter of the directness of their contact with the environment, for which they would serve as a kind of conduit. Rather, the determinacy is a property of the mode by which the environment is represented.

I have suggested that what that means is that for some tasks, the kinds of perceptual categories supplied by displaylike mental structures are more adequate than those contained in Pylyshyn's model. Nondiscursive structures are more determinate, in some cases, because they serve to determine more effectively the object of vision. But, it is important to note, there is no single way in which this is so. One might think that the virtue of percepts and images lies in the wealth of details they provide, recalling naturally the old adage about a picture being worth a thousand words. It is crucial to see that, while it can be important, perceptual determinateness need not consist essentially in just that sort of richness.

As will become clear in the next chapter, there is a variety of image types that differ in the extent to which they represent details. Indeed, overlooking that fact has been the source of one misguided line of disparagement of the pictorialist model of imagery. Thus, I want to suggest that what might be called the referential effectiveness of mental displays is due to a number of distinctive characteristics of the type of categorial and selective functions they serve: open-endedness of perceptual categories, visual orientation ability, holistic representation, refinement and weighting of details, as well as inclusion of incidental information about relations among features.

Ultimately, accounting for these functions will raise the issue of how to assign *content* to perceptual beliefs. Since that problem is generalizable, it points to a much larger question about the semantic properties of propositional attitudes of all kinds. Because the issue goes beyond the concern here with perceptual reference, I want to postpone further discussion of it until later.

There is, however, a particular problem that has become the focus of concern lately. That is the problem of knowledge representation. The argument is that no set of singular propositions and computations defined over them will suffice to explain how we can comprehend the information with which we are confronted, in a complex environment through which we must learn to make our way.

Earlier I suggested that there are certain tasks—for example, the recognition of a face in a crowded room—for which a finite list of features would be inadequate. That point can be extended to question the adequacy of the procedures that would employ such a list or set of descriptions. An argument can be made that those procedures need a guiding structure to orient them, as it were, to the environment in which they are employed. For example, Hilary Putnam and Hubert Dreyfus have explicitly linked the need for holistic and concrete analog operations to the concern to locate mental activity within a larger context; and a natural inference would be that nonpropositional images can provide orientation to the context by way of their determinate representational character. Since the issue arises in conjunction with arguments for the nature of knowledge representation, it is a problem deserving special attention. It also bears directly on the status of skills and creative ability as capacities of a possibly cognitive sort.

KNOWLEDGE REPRESENTATION, INSIGHT, AND SKILL

In essence, the problem of knowledge representation is how to explain the way in which an intelligent system, in performing cognitive tasks, detects and organizes the relevant information from the multifarious sensory input with which it is bombarded. This problem has two related dimensions: to explicate the form or structure that knowledge has, or must have, given the nature of one task or another; and to explain how that form or structure is especially sensitive to those features of a situation that are relevant to some task. How does the mind select and attend to the information it needs and filter out what it does not need for a particular kind of task, in a world over-rich with potentially informative stimuli?

We need a model both holistic and active. In order to negotiate the surrounding and incoming mélange of information, we need forms that represent larger sets of data than the atomistic subject-property relations of singular propositions taken one at a time. Further, it would seem that a condition on the ability to cope with novel and diverse stimuli—a capacity that is in fact characteristic of natural intelligence—is active engagement and testing rather than mere passive receptivity.

A number of efforts have been made recently to satisfy this condition in artificial intelligence research, notably by Marvin Minsky, Roger Schank, and Terry Winograd. Each has introduced a means by which to represent stereotypical situations (frames, scripts, and multidimensional prototypes, respectively) to which a computer can be programmed to respond.[13]

A frame, for example, is essentially just that, a framework into which input can be fitted, an open-ended description of a stereotypical situation that, by virtue of what it says, constitutes an expectation of the kind of further information that will be coming in to complete it. So, for example, one such situation might be a "room," a description which implies the discovery, on further perception, of a rectangular shape, four flat walls, and then perhaps details like doors and windows. A frame thus tells us something, but not everything, about what to expect in exploring a situation. It implies, in that respect, a set of questions about a particular kind of situation and the appropriate response to it; it is, we might say, not a complete description of a scene (which would be impossible) but a description of it from a point of view, that is, as a scene of a certain type. It is thus a kind of hypothetical perspective on the world, which must be tested as more information comes in.

It is important to keep in mind what this adds to the basic "semantic engine" model. Fodor and others have argued that thoughts take the form of mental sentences as hypotheses about one's present and future perceptual state. But, for the most part, the testing of representations of that sort is a matter of trying to develop their logical relations to other mental sentences that can be computed. But frames are supposed to be rather different, in two senses: (a) they leave open initially some aspects of the described situation (that is, they do not entail an explicit rule for the thought "There is a room"), and (b) the testing of them is not just a matter of working out their logical relations to other sentences or frames. Minsky argues in fact that a different kind of reasoning is involved in the use of frames, one which depends on recognizing similarities in scenes; and that involves reasoning by analogy. This is necessary, Minsky argues, because traditional deductive and inductive logic are not very effective in coping with realistic, complicated problems. To solve such problems, it is essential to be able to represent approximations to solutions, and the traditional model is not very well suited to that purpose.

In the case of linguistic usage, we thus need something more than syntactical forms and semantic properties. We need something like typical story plots or, as Minsky calls them, "narrative frames," or scenarios. Interconnections between story elements help bridge gaps that logic finds hard to cross. A narrative or story is not just a set of logically connected descriptions; rather it has a structure that affects the meaning of any sentence within it. And, presumably, the value of that lies in the fact that real world history (even that of an individual life) has a kind of narrative structure: It fits together (as it is represented, at least) into a more or less coherent story. Thus mental narrative frames, basic story plots, should be very helpful in negotiating the real temporal world.

This is where Schank comes in. His modification of frame theory is specifically in terms of what he calls "scripts," which are supposed to enable computers to understand simple stories, in particular about stereotypical social situations like ordering a meal in a restaurant. Here the computer can respond appropriately to somewhat diverse inputs, because it knows something of how the story is supposed to go in that context.

What is distinctive about frames and scripts are the procedures they allow to be implemented. These procedures are defined over descriptions. Nonetheless, it is clear that Minsky wants to describe frames as mental representations that are in some sense concrete and, in that respect, imagelike. Thus he quotes the early work of the psychologist F. C. Bartlett, on what the latter called "schemata": "Thinking . . . is biologically subsequent to the image-forming process. . . . But . . . it does not supercede the method of images."[14] And these schemata Minsky explicitly relates to what Thomas Kuhn has called paradigms. But this comparison has made Minsky vulnerable to the criticism that he fails to carry his program far enough. Indeed, Dreyfus has argued vigorously, no program can satisfy the concerns that motivate the development of semiholistic modes of representation, and that reveals the limits of artificial intelligence.

What Minsky forgets, Dreyfus argues, is just how concrete paradigms are supposed to be. A paradigm is "*not* an abstract explicit descriptive scheme utilizing formal features," which is basically what Minsky's frames are, despite disclaimers about avoiding abstractness, but rather "a shared concrete case, which dispenses with features altogether."[15]

Whether this is precisely Kuhn's meaning or not, Dreyfus focuses on the idea that the relevant concreteness can be provided by images in a nonpropositional form. Thus he cites with approval the work of Eleanor Rosch on perceptual prototypes. Rosch says, for example, "The most cognitively economical code for a category is, in fact, a concrete image of an average category member."[16] Although Rosch's prototypes are not necessarily restricted to images in a nonlinguistic form, the point is that she opens the door, at least, to useful research about the role of such images. What Dreyfus argues is that, as more psychologists begin to investigate "the function of images as opposed to symbolic representations, the strikingly limited success of AI may come to be seen as an important disconfirmation of the information processing model."[17]

Putnam has expressed similar reservations. Although he does not explicitly connect the two points, he concedes that the mind may work like an analog processor in some cases; and he argues that, insofar as cognitive psychology depends upon the model of the digital computer, it will not be able to account for many kinds of important contextual factors.[18]

The critical assumption is that the function of images is "opposed to [that of] symbolic representations." Images are, for Dreyfus, "nonformal representations," by which he means that they are not governed by explicit rules and conditions for use and interpretation. I think that the deficits Dreyfus points out in these other models are real concerns; but I want to argue that some assumptions on which his analysis of images rests are unwarranted. To see this we must consider the notion of a prototype on which he draws.

One virtue of concentrating on prototype theory is that it brings out the ways in which typicality, and hence similarity, plays a role in the models proposed by Minsky, Schank, and Winograd, as well as in the work of Rosch. This theory contrasts significantly with the more traditional view that, in order to recognize different kinds of objects, people have to be able to classify them under some particular concept or set of related concepts. Concepts function like abstract rules for identifying a perceptual object as one sort of thing or another, say, a bird as distinct from a basketball. These rules lay down, as it were, necessary and sufficient conditions for anything to count as a bird-appearance; it is necessary, say, for it to have wings, and it is sufficient if it has feathers.

Prototypes, on the other hand, do *not* function like abstract rules that set necessary and sufficient conditions on the categories of the perceptual world. Rather, they function like concrete exemplars or paradigms for things of the relevant category, to which we match the visual stimuli. Objects are grouped according to how similar or different they are from an imagined or remembered paradigm. Rosch has shown, for example, that people can recognize more easily (that is, more quickly on a statistical average) a robin as a bird than they recognize a chicken as a bird.[19] Why should this be so? If the *concept* of a bird implies necessary and sufficient conditions for being a bird, and both of them have the features that satisfy those conditions, should they not be equally easy to put into the relevant category? According to Rosch, the answer must be that robins and chickens are compared to a bird prototype when they are seen; and robins are more similar to it.

To support the claim that such categorization can be understood in terms of the employment of concrete, nonlinguistic prototypes, several considerations may be cited. First, the mere fact that the use of concrete mental forms might be rule governed does not necessarily violate their status as analogs, exemplars, or prototypes, which themselves do not specify necessary and sufficient conditions. There could be rules for determining the degree to which an object is similar to a prototype, even though the prototype itself is not an explicit rule for saying when an object does or does not satisfy the conditions for falling into one category or another. This is basically like saying that there can be rules, indeed that there can be algorithmic procedures, for implementing heuristic strategies, even though the strategies themselves are essentially rules of thumb rather than step-by-step procedures. In any case, establishing the controversial claim that prototypes are unlike concepts that provide necessary and sufficient conditions for object recognition is not part of my project. What matters is that the vocabulary of available prototypes, identified as figural displays, systematically constrains the further construction of images. I will show how that might work in the next chapter.

Second, as part of his critique of Schank's notion of scripts, Dreyfus argues that the notion is too artificial because it relies on the assumption that one can designate some actions as primitive, and there are no primitive actions per se, that is, which are primitive for all accounts. Read Kierkegaard's several variations on the story of the sacrifice of Isaac, for example, and you will quickly realize that an action that is primitive, that is, basic, in one version (say Abraham's raising his arm in a certain way to strike Isaac) is taken in another version to be highly expressive and complex, the product of other simple, primitive acts. Furthermore, any set of primitive actions for the actors in the script, or any set of frames or prototypes, will necessarily be finite. Therefore, there will be a definite limit on the ability of a system that employs them to respond to novelty, to new situations. But we humans seem to have no limits, except qualitative ones, in that regard. The conclusion Dreyfus would like to draw, then, is that frames and scripts cannot be adequate models for natural intelligence.

This point about the finiteness of the vocabulary for script construction can be generalized to apply to any form of knowledge representation, no matter how concrete. However, the attempt to apply it generally would have to rest on a false presupposition. The capacity of humans to respond to novelty is, to a large extent, due to the fact that our language is such that it permits endless combinations of a finite vocabulary according to rules. The general critique of various forms of knowledge representation must, in light of that, assume that there can be no generative grammar of prototypes, frames, or other stereotypes. Insofar as prototypes are thought to be concrete, nonlinguistic images, there is some precedent for this view. However, it is an assumption that must be justified; and I will argue specifically against it in the next chapters.

In any case, such a rule-following capability would defeat the purpose of nonformal representation for Dreyfus. A representation of that sort is one way in which we can comprehend the world in which we live; and that is, for him, a comprehension that is logically antecedent to theoretical knowledge. This comprehension is a kind of skill acquired by experience; it need not itself be represented. It is, however, possible to reflect on how it is exercised; and for that, the image is of value. I can use "nonformal representations, more like images, by means of which I explore what I am, not what I know."[20]

This possibility opens the door to an understanding of the creative insight that computers appear to lack. One approach to an account of creativity is to treat it as an ability of a certain sort. For example, as Haugeland puts it, there is the ability to recognize that a scientific or philosophical theory or an overall logical strategy is reasonable, "the ability to tell when a whole account, a whole way of putting things, makes sense."[21] It is not at all clear that a computer model that employs nothing but structured descriptions can provide for this capacity.

Computational creativity would seem to consist in this: There will be a rationale for relating changes in "theory" to antecedent capacities, that is, for connecting new behavior to prior typical patterns of response; thus, the very nature of "insight" will be endemically conservative. Prospective changes in a program will be assessed relative to the rules for systematic change already incorporated in it. That amounts to judging novel stimuli that might threaten the apparent sensibility of the overall framework by constructing a rationale to accommodate them. The presuppositions upon which the construction itself is based would not themselves be threatened. In effect, Dreyfus deals with that problem by attaching priority to experience with the world. Such experience can produce a kind of competence that is independent of the ability to represent that world. Since representational ability depends upon the development of this experiential competence, and since that development presupposes no antecedent theory or program to guide it, the result is that cognition is no longer stultified. Indeed, cognitive ability itself becomes a kind of skill.

This is a view shared by others. Richard Rorty, for example, has suggested that, if there were internal representations, facility with them would be a fundamental skill.[22] In a certain respect, the manipulation of symbols can be understood to require something like pattern recognition, and pattern recognition is a skill that is not explained by postulating an internal label or quasi-linguistic representation, because the question remains about how the ability to apply the label is acquired or in what it consists. This is essentially an argument for something very much like the basic imaging capacity discussed in the first chapter. Recently, in fact, Howard Margolis has argued that pattern recognition is basic to all cognition and that it is alogical.[23] I agree that it is basic; however, to construe it as altogether alogical is a fundamental mistake. Rather, that capacity must be understood in terms of conformity to rules, at least, if it is to be invoked as a ground for representational competence. Since the argument to the contrary assumes that what is presupposed is a skill, which does not depend upon knowledge representation, a closer look at the nature of skills is in order.

One well-known argument for the view that skills are not represented comes, of course, from Gilbert Ryle. With regard to mental imagery in particular, Ryle declared, "I want to show that the concept of picturing, visualizing or 'seeing' is a proper and useful concept, but that its use does not entail the existence of a gallery in which such pictures are ephemerally suspended." On his view, "imaging occurs, but images are not seen," in the sense that having a mental image "is actually a special case of imagining, namely imagining that we see."[24] As a type of covert "pretending," imagining requires refraining from overt behavior; but it is an ability that presupposes perceptual knowledge, that is, knowledge of what it would be like to see whatever it is one imagines.

This knowledge is not propositional. One can pretend to do something by miming it, even though one cannot describe it; and one can understand a description of an activity without being able to imitate it. For example, I can read and understand instructions or see and comprehend a diagram of movements and still not know what a dance routine looks like. Nor is visualizing a routine a matter of seeing a mental diagram or reading a mental description of it; rather, for Ryle it is to know what it would be like to see the routine, but to refrain from exercising the dispositions that define that knowledge. Whatever those dispositions are, they do not constitute a "knowing that" something is the case. Knowing the principles of balance or being able to articulate grammatical rules does not constitute proficiency on a bicycle or linguistic competence. Thus, Ryle's analysis of imaging is a natural extension of his general critique of what he called the "intellectualist legend." The exercise of various skills and abilities depends upon nonpropositional knowledge; and visualization itself is a kind of "know how."

Ryle's insight is that imaging exploits perceptual knowledge not exhausted by a process of description and inference. But Ryle was concerned to establish the logical dependence of *all* mental activity upon the behavioral capacities of the agent, so as to avoid a separate category of ghostly apparitions that must be examined internally to ascertain their content. Knowledge is not represented, he argues, in the sense that would require a relation between a person and a set of mental symbols. A symbol can always represent both more and less than is known by the subject in whose thoughts it occurs; but imagining and other forms of thinking are epistemic activities, wholly constituted by what the subject knows.[25]

The problem is that the dispositions relevant to a behavioristic account of imagining are a mystery; and the notion of nonpropositional knowledge that is not in any way represented is an uncertain notion at best. There are, in fact, some very interesting recent empirical studies supporting the claim that imagery is employed in the exercise of skills.[26] And the inadequacy of inferences defined over mental sentences becomes particularly apparent in the exercise of skills, where motor responses must be very quick, a considerable amount of diverse information must be accessed simultaneously, continuity and flow from one state to another are important, and subtle adaptations and modifications of rules are required for excellence in performance. But how is the requisite knowledge accessed? The importance of minute but crucial variations, for example, in a gymnastics exercise, surely undermines the view that no access is needed, on the grounds that the performance is virtually automatic. To be sure, one need not think about textbook typing instructions to produce a typed text; but that does not mean that principles of performance must not be encoded in some other way. It would simply be begging the question to deny that skillful behavior is intelligent in some sense. That there are standards by which success is gauged, that improvement is possible, that there are stages among which cogent connections obtain, all suggest that, while skillful knowledge may be nonpropositional, it is nonetheless knowledge that is represented mentally.

EMOTIONS AND MOODS

The importance of motor responses in the exercise of skills suggests that they are to be understood in part as physiological in nature. That is, if the analysis of the preceding section is right, the concept of a skill implies that there are two integrated dimensions to skillful behavior, the cognitive and the physical. The dual dimension of skills provides an important point of contact with emotion, insofar as the tendency to view emotion as having a cognitive function as well as a physical basis is correct. Moreover, a characteristic sometimes attributed to skills as well as to emotions and moods is their essential nonlocalizability. An ability, one might argue, is not a bit of knowledge located somewhere inside someone's head. Similarly, emotions and moods tend to be pervasive; they affect the whole person's general outlook and behavior. There is thus something comprehensive about them.

Grounding emotions in biological processes would be an appealing way to account for the fact that emotional effects can be systematically suffused, for it would seem to capture something that an exclusively propositional computer model leaves out, namely, the "visceral" dimension of feelings and emotion. Cognitive science is virtually defined by its commitment to there being an unbreakable explanatory bond between belief and desires; yet it is the beliefs that have gotten almost all of the good press. Of course, desire has sometimes surfaced, disguised as a preference function, which can be defined over sentential states. But that hardly seems sufficient to account for all that we mean when we speak of objects of desire. Perhaps Don Giovanni's desire for Donna Anna should be understood as a desire that a certain sentence be true, a sentence about Don Giovanni's embrace of that particular woman. But an account connecting that, in a systematic way, with the biological urge that lies behind it would be much more gratifying.

Of course, it would be a mistake to conclude on the basis of their pervasive and visceral character that emotions and moods are entirely noncognitive. It has been a concern from early on to show that a generally functionalist account of the mind, operating under the influence of the computational model, can accommodate nonoccurrent features that are not localizable as logical states. The strategy has been to attribute them to the overall organization of the system. The network of relations among mental states will itself exhibit certain features that are whole-system, pervasive properties. And, as I have suggested, the account is compatible with the attribution of a qualitative character to mental states by way of the biological processes that instantiate them. I want to argue that this account works better when it is taken to include nonpropositional images. Insofar as such images are shown to have a cognitive function, they are much better suited to capture the dual physiological-cognitive character of emotion. There is a hint that this is so in the intuitive likelihood that a picture can provoke passion more easily than a description.[27]

Cognitive theories of emotion generally assume that the cognitive dimension of emotion comes from its connection to beliefs and preferences. The connection is taken to be either a causal relation, a logical dependence, or a partial constitutiveness. Emotions can supervene on physiological processes by way of their connections to supervenient belief representations, thus joining the physiological and the cognitive components and acquiring a rationality parasitic on that of belief. In this way, emotions come to exhibit intentionality.[28] If that is so, however, it remains to be said precisely how different relations among representations of beliefs and preferences work either to cause or constitute various kinds of emotion. In giving such an account, what will be required is not simply a connection between emotions and beliefs but a connection of those to nonpropositional images.

Historically, cognitive theories of emotion have been distinguished from expression theories, which identify emotions in behavioral terms. However, it is possible to understand the cognitive function of emotions in terms of the expressiveness of mental representations, the dynamics of which constitute a kind of internal behavior. For example, Haugeland has suggested that there could be a sentential model that captures the way moods and emotions permeate and affect a wide variety of cognitive states. Moods and emotions, he suggests, can be explained by sentential states that are integrated into a format not like the sequential processing of a computer but rather like a novel, that is, a linguistic genre in which words are used in more than a descriptive fashion: "It would be like an exciting or depressing chapter in a novel; the characterization does not apply to any particular sentence or to any specifiable structure of sentences, and yet there is nothing on the page but ordered sentences."[29]

There have been, of course, a number of attempts recently to make use of textual models for explanation in the social sciences. Further, Arthur Danto and Jerome Bruner have suggested that the mind in particular is like a text in certain respects.[30] These are fertile ideas, though it remains to be seen whether they are actually incompatible with the computer model altogether. To be sure, while a computer enacts Schank's scripts as a kind of mechanical storyteller, it is no modern Homer. Rather, the robotic rhapsodist tells tales that are entirely formulaic. What was for the great Greek poet merely a framework on which to hang his notorious similes is for the computer the whole story. Nonetheless, the issue is still open whether there can be programmable principles of composition or, to put it the other way around, whether narration can be construed as a cognitive process. Rorty, for one, has argued that the mastery of metaphor and other literary devices is a skill and thus not a kind of knowledge representable in a computer's program. As the preceding section shows, however, if it is a skill, that alone will not suffice to segregate it from the realm of mental representation.

This is a matter that will surface again later, when the role of images in visual narrative is discussed. However, putting aside the larger question of the relevance of textual models in general for cognitive psychology, the point to note here is that Haugeland's claim that emotion can be captured by a wholly sentential model, by virtue of the expressiveness of certain sets of sentences, is not entirely convincing. There is, of course, nothing comparable in a novel to the effects of moods upon perception and behavior, since, after all, texts do not perceive and behave. The expressiveness of a story depends upon the sensitivities of the author and the reader, which themselves must be explained by a psychological account. This suggests that the internal analog will have to consist in some further "interpretation" of sets of sentences, in the form of operations defined, not just over sentences taken individually but over relations among them.

It is thus important to point out that there is a traditional account in aesthetic psychology of Haugeland's proposed model; and it employs mental images that are pictorial in nature. There is precedent in both philosophy and psychology for the view that emotional expressiveness in general and the functions of various tropes in particular depend upon the generation of visual images in the mind of the reader or listener. These images carry emotional content, having been associated in the past with other images produced on the occasion of some immediate feelings. If the entire process of image production in response to words is taken to be internal, so that the words in question are mental sentences, the implication is that emotion is due to the expressiveness of the verbal thought by way of the visual image.

The model of expressiveness employed here is, of course, not uncontroversial. The main problem with invoking it in support of the link between emotional expressiveness and imagery is that the early accounts that draw upon it are derived, for the most part, from associationist or Gestalt psychology. While both of these have been rehabilitated recently, it is important to articulate a theory of how images function symbolically in a representational system to establish initially their cognitive credentials.

In developing an account of the cognitive function of images, the theory must address three points. How, precisely, does the image generate emotion? How is it connected to the relevant linguistic representation? And what is the cognitive value of emotions so produced? With regard to the last point, apart from attempts going back to Aristotle to show that there is a "logic" of emotion, another, indirect argument can be given: If imagery can be shown to play a central role in the generation of emotion, and if imagery can be further shown to function cognitively, then at least part of the cognitive value of emotion can be said to derive from the function of the image.

One interesting approach that has obvious points of contact with the earlier discussion of knowledge representation has been proposed by Ronald de Sousa. As he notes, the view that emotions are judgments assumes that "only propositional attitudes of the kinds familiar from the formulation of beliefs and desires can be assessed for rationality," and that assumption is false. Inference to true belief is but one species of transition, the adequacy of which can be assessed in terms of its probability of success. De Sousa claims that a condition on emotions is their appropriateness to a given situation, and he tries to develop standards by introducing "paradigm scenarios" that provide both objects and typical emotional responses. Since he defines emotions as determinate "patterns of salience among objects of attention, lines of inquiry, and inferential analyses," developing a repertoire of paradigm scenarios would be tantamount to defining appropriateness conditions on emotions.[31]

This is in some ways similar to the analysis I will give of the rationality of images, which was developed independently. The notion of "appropriateness conditions" is, of course, entirely general and applicable to a variety of phenomena. However, there are two ways in which I would argue de Sousa's account is incomplete and, in particular, in need of a theory of the role of imagery in emotion. First, something needs to be said about the psychological form that patterns of salience take. In his discussion of functionalism and the emotions, Georges Rey states well the central thesis of computational functionalism: "What is rational seems to be representational; what is representational, formal; and what is formal . . . seems to be most perspicuously understood algorithmically."[32] If the notion of a formal algorithm is not taken in too austere a fashion to require propositions, it is right to assume a connection between rationality and representation. Since patterns of salience are not propositional attitudes, some other mode of representation is required. Further, the appropriateness of emotions on de Sousa's account will be relative to a social context. In keeping with the computational model, Rey suggests that the Wittgensteinian concern for context, a concern which emerged clearly in the arguments of Dreyfus and Putnam, may be best satisfied in terms of an account of the relations among mental states. This view will become much more plausible when the relations include nonpropositional images. As de Sousa points out, some situations demand complex linguistic skills to produce their full emotional effects. I would argue that the derivation of patterns of salience from paradigm scenes requires in many cases, perhaps most, complex perceptual and pictorial skills for their emotional effect, as well.

Second, establishing a relation between a situation in which there are patterns of salience and a "formal object," that is, the quality associated with the paradigm, is very much like establishing a relation between an expressive set of representations and an image with which emotion is associated. What replaces the image is a more holistic, comprehensive, orienting frame; but the argument has been made that such devices should be construed as at least imagelike. That possibility adds weight to de Sousa's suggestion that the formal object in this case might also be the intentional object.

The role of nonpropositional imagery in establishing perceptual determinacy and contextual orientation, in the exercise of skills and in the generation of emotion, depends upon judgments of typicality and similarity; and that, I want to argue, is a virtue. The relation of such judgments to attributions of propositional attitudes to oneself and others, and to the assessment of rationality that such attributions imply, has lately been the source of much controversy. Grounding the judgments on imagery, I will argue, leads to a clearer and more substantive theory that sheds helpful light on those controversies.

However, it must first be shown *how* images and other nonpropositional forms of knowledge representation can be employed to constitute judgments. Granting that they are different from the kind of computation and inference defined over descriptions, it is clear that some account must be given of how they are to be interpreted. What sort of account that should be, I want to show, is not obvious. The problem of interpretation becomes acute when the fact is confronted that there is actually a variety of image types.

What the considerations here have suggested is a point for which I will argue both more directly and more generally in ensuing sections: a considerable amount of the behavior we consider intelligent requires a plurality of modes of mental representation, and often the functions of those modes necessarily intersect. The point is illustrated, metaphorically at least, by the case of Dr. P. What is lacking in Dr. P., and in theories of cognition in general, is not the visual schema by which to encode perceptual features, but the capacity to fit them into a system of beliefs, desires, and characteristic views of the visual world.

Seeing a set of features—a mustache, a jaw, a smile—as his brother Paul is what Dr. P. could not do. What he could do was infer from them that Paul was there. Believing is not seeing; and this suggests that vision and visualization cannot be reduced to relations among propositional attitudes. When Dr. P. mistook his wife for a hat, he did not see her as one; rather, he just drew the wrong conclusion—he made a logical mistake. And Oliver Sacks is right: We should try to avoid making a similar mistake. But an aversion to what amount to rules for visual representation, I think, is wrong. It produces a kind of skepticism about the possibility of a science of the mind; and skepticism about a complete science of the mind is important, because it amounts to skepticism about science as such. The implication is that the effort to account for all the facts of the matter is bound to fail. And that is a conclusion not to be drawn too quickly. The "romantic science," as A. R. Luria called the neuropsychology of right hemispheric functions, could after all be a science.

CHAPTER FOUR

Intentional Icons

The Problem of Interpretation

Thirty years ago, J. M. Shorter noted that images are typically said to have some of the properties of pictures, some of the features of descriptions, and some characteristics attributable to both. Thus he was led to suggest that mental images inhabit "a sort of half-way house between pictures and descriptions"; and insofar as they are like pictures, "it seems that they can be regarded in two ways, as objects in their own right as well as representations of other things."[1]

In Shorter's case, however, the apparent introduction of a medium of mental representation is only a manner of speaking. Indeed, for him, it is both "a logical and an empirical fact" that "mental images do not exist."[2] To refer to a mental image as a depiction or a description is merely a verbal convenience.

Nonetheless, in some ways Shorter's claim anticipates an important line of argument in cognitive psychology, exemplified by Fodor's identification of a continuum of types of representation ranging from "photographs to paragraphs."[3] The importance of the introduction of a continuum is twofold. First, it supports the idea that it would be a mistake to drive a methodological wedge between explanation in terms of operations on images and that in terms of proposition-based computational procedures. Second, it suggests a theoretical framework within which to account for the conjunction of pictures and propositions. If there is a continuum of types of representation, the obvious question to ask is, what are the dimensions along which it varies? What are the properties shared by the various types, in virtue of which they are all said to be representations? Presumably there is a sense in which they must have a capacity for content. In that case, we are faced with two possibilities. Either content in each instance is essentially derivative from some basic function, and the differences are only superficial, or there are some genuinely different modes of representation, albeit with overlapping characteristics. In either case, we will want to know what determines the differences as well as the similarities.

There is thus a prima facie problem of distinguishing among types of representation. How exactly, one wants to know, is a map different from a photograph? This is of course a problem that has perplexed a number of philosophers with regard to physical images. As it turns out, an answer suggests itself naturally, namely, that the differences are largely due to the *interpretations* under which images are brought. This suggestion is natural because the need for interpretation cuts across image type categories. Furthermore, there is a legitimate and important sense in which even mental sentences must be brought under interpretation, that is, in their linkage to other sentences in computational processes.

Nonetheless, it is much too easy to slip into thinking that it is their conjunction with sentences that provides the interpretation for any kind of image and, indeed, that what a sentence says about the image is what makes it the particular type of image that it is. Two considerations suggest that this is a mistake. First, it will soon become clear that near the middle of the spectrum, displays and descriptions of information taken together constitute certain kinds of representation. In those cases, they are mutually dependent; thus no special weight should be assigned to the propositional component. The display determines the content of the description—hence, interprets it—as much as the description determines the character of the display. And the fact that these cases are continuous with other types nearer the end of the spectrum suggests that this interdependence is a feature of the family of image types, which varies by degree.

Second, there is another prima facie problem brought on by the appeal to interpretation of images in determining their types; and that is the problem of how to account for the relations between the various displays and their descriptions. There is, in other words, the problem of the interpretation relation itself. Why this is a problem can be seen by taking Fodor's analysis as illustrative of a general line of thought. Fodor argues that there will be the need to provide for interpretation in any system that includes images. Images cannot function alone because no iconic system could provide the key to its own grammatical structure. In such a system, for example, a picture of a cat located above a log might be taken to mean "The cat is on the log," whereas a picture of a log located above a cat would mean "The cat is under the log." However, such pictorial representations would be inherently ambiguous. The first could also mean "The log is under the cat," or even "The cat is sleeping like a log!" The principles of pictorial representation, whatever they are, do not permit the representation of determinate thoughts.

Nonetheless it might be thought that, while pictures could not function like sentences, they might function like words and, more particularly, like names: "If Iconic English were the language of thought, then thinking of John might consist of entertaining John's image; just as, in the standard use of ordinary English, mentioning John (referring to him) might just consist in uttering John's name." Thus, images could be used to refer to things, but only when they are "taken under" descriptions. To return to an example introduced earlier: "So one might say 'I am looking for a man who looks like this ...' and show a picture of a man.... The form of words wouldn't usually succeed in communicating a reference unless the picture of the man looks like the man one is seeking.... What carries reference here is the picture together with the 'symbols' that interpret it."[4]

It is clear, as I noted earlier, that the issue here is the capacity to refer and not any actual referential use. In this case, the picture is introduced because its formal features enhance that capacity. The central question then is, What is the precise nature of the relation between the two formal types?

Fodor explains how word-symbols and pictures are brought together in terms that suggest that the pictures literally fill in blanks in the sentences: "There is, in fact, a perfectly good way of using a picture to make a reference, viz. by embedding it in a description."[5] Invoking the notion of embedding implies that the linguistic representation is, in effect, incomplete without the picture to play some grammatical role. However, this cannot be exactly the right interpretation for two reasons. First, it would then not be strictly correct to speak of bringing a picture under or together with a description, since prior to its pictorial impregnation, the linguistic entity would not be well formed and hence would not *be* a description. Further, this conception of the role of imagery in thought would disregard characteristics that facilitate certain tasks. When Fodor discusses the flexibility of the mental representational system, he suggests that the image, *rather than* the description, may be used to do perceptual categorization simultaneously rather than in a series. This implies that the image is not literally a component within the linguistic formula.[6]

Thus it is more appropriate to think of the image as coexisting with a description that refers to it, as well as to the object whose identity the image helps establish. But in that case, whatever structure the image has is not simply attributed to it by the interpretation. If it were, one image would be as good as another, and any interpretation would be wholly arbitrary. The image is supposed to have enough formal organization, on this theory, to impose some constraints on its adaptation for certain tasks; but if it is to impose constraints, that organization or structure must be accessible in a way that is antecedent to the image being brought under a description.[7] What might be called the problem of mental *ekphrasis* cannot be satisfactorily resolved without presupposing that the object of ekphrasis has a determinate structure of its own. To account for the very nature of the nonarbitrary links between propositions and pictures, it must be possible in principle to identify an internal vocabulary of sorts for pictures.[8] With regard to the spectrum of representational types, this means that their variety is not simply the product of interpretation. The possibility of modes of interpretation depends upon it. Indeed, the very existence of a variety of modes lends intuitive force to the argument. If there were no intrinsic differences between photographs and stick figures, for example, each should work equally well with precisely the same description for any task. The implausibility of that result is apparent.

That is not to say of course that what distinguishes, for example, a prototype from a caricature, is never, in any respect, an interpretation. Surely it is; but there is a further point I wish to establish in that regard. The interpretation of displayed information need not consist in appending to it a verbal description that gives it a more determinate content. It can consist, rather, in a series of modifications of the display itself.

This is a possibility that is not at all trivial. Indeed, it flies in the face of considerations that have led to what Daniel Dennett has called scientific "iconophobia."[9] In the earlier discussion of methodological constraints, we saw that the argument that operations on images should be treated as noncognitive was predicated on a certain assumption, namely, that any structure that might be imputed to nonpropositional images would not be the sort appropriate to the conveyance of semantic properties. That argument would, of course, be self-serving if it simply took for granted that the only genuine semantic properties were linguistic. But to show that there might be other kinds of semantic properties is no easy task. The accounts of syntax and semantics generally go hand in hand; and, on the model of mental representation I have been assuming, those accounts cannot be separated from an account of the processes in which representations play a part.

In order to lay the groundwork for a theory about the syntactical and semantical properties of nonpropositional images, I want to explore first some of the ways in which various kinds of images combine visual and verbal information. The point will be both to show that the visual component plays an essential role and to illustrate generally how it does it. I then want to introduce a more specific formal mechanism as the means by which nonpropositional images are constructed and to ground it on certain principles. What that grounding will make clear is the primary importance of visual semantic properties for any pictorialist theory of mental imagery. Those properties will be defined procedurally to some extent here and further in the next chapter. I will argue there that the procedures in question cannot be understood in terms of relations among belief and desire, the two stalwarts of representational psychology. The result will be the addition of a new category to the explanation of intelligent behavior.

MIXED MEDIA
Varieties of Imagistic Representation

As Fodor has noted, not all images are pictorial, even though they are accessed visually. A nondiscursive representation is simply one in which "the information is displayed rather than described."[10] For example, the line representing the equator on a map does not look like the equator region; but the map displays its information about the equator nonetheless. The shapes and relative sizes of continents may be somewhat more similar to the features of the objects they represent, but only minimally so compared to a photograph as a "paradigmatic" image.

Thus images, in Fodor's analysis, can vary in the degree to which they resemble their objects. The possibility of this continuum shows a weakness in one argument for descriptionalism. Dennett, for example, claims that images are *indeterminate,* whereas pictures are not; therefore, images must have a "descriptional character."[11] But as Fodor notes, it is not true that every image must be determinate under such descriptions as "has *n* stripes" (where the image is, say, of a striped tiger); it must only be determinate under *some* visual description. In other words, nondiscursive representations need not be determinate for every perceptible property.

Indeterminacy can, of course, take several forms. For example, prototypical or schematic representations omit particular details by virtue of their organizational features, that is, the arrangement of lines and parts. In this respect, they obviously differ from the omission of details from descriptions. Linguistic indeterminacy is not a function of the number and arrangement of parts: fewer words do not necessarily diminish detail. Moreover, sometimes successful schematization is patently a reflection of a representational technique, defined in terms of skill in manipulating the medium.

Imagine, for example, a simple line drawing of a human figure in which the circle defining the head is wobbly on one side. If it is a poor drawing, the pathology of representation is not apparent because of any dissimilarity between it and a human head. Well-defined circularity is not a feature of real heads. It is a feature of schematic representations of heads that, in effect, abstract from individual differences. In this case, what is pathological in one case can be normal form in another, for example, if the drawing is a caricature, for which wobbly lines are appropriate. What then is required to make the distinction?

One clue lies in the other dimension along which Fodor suggests image types may vary. He says that the "intermediate cases are, in effect, images under descriptions; they convey some information discursively and some information pictorially, and they resemble their subjects only in respect of those properties that happen to be pictured."[12] The precise form that this progression takes toward greater discursiveness, in the movement from photographs to paragraphs, is hard to make clear. A serious descriptionalist will maintain that even a detailed photograph will require interpretation by a description. But presumably the point is that, in fact, photographs do not normally come with labels as constituents. Maps and graphs do, and unlike the latter, descriptions are not constituted, even in part, by displays (though they may be sometimes aided by an added illustration or two). Thus, even nonpictorial images require interpretation; but in certain cases like maps and graphs, descriptive markers are partly constitutive of the representation itself.

I want to suggest, however, that in the case of these displays it is especially clear that the description would be insufficient by itself. For example, although maps require latitude and longitude lines, the shapes and relative sizes of continents and relative locations of cities, however unlike the real geography they may be, serve as an index for the application of a rule like "* denotes a capital city."

Consider, as another example, a curve in a graph line. Since the curve is drawn to show a trend based upon some data, its appropriateness is relative to the data from which it draws its hypothetical projection. But the situation is not that simple; the very arc of the curve, which proceeds on its set course, may determine what data are "anomalous" and, thus, to be discarded. That is, while a curve may be epiphenomenal to the mathematical computation of locations, it may also be functional: It may reflect the effects of habit or chance, or a simplicity criterion can be approximated by following the natural flow of the line. That is tantamount to visual computation.

These examples illustrate ways in which the formal features of an image can be understood to possess an inherent definition that justifies their conjunction with a particular sentence.[13] But there is, as I have suggested, a further point that emerges from these examples. Not only can we find in them a relation of mutual dependence between display and description; these "intermediate" modes of representation also exemplify a specifiable relation between the display component and its object.

To see how, we can consider the fact that Fodor and others have argued that perception, as well as action and learning, require formulating hypotheses and confirming them. Confirmation depends, in part, upon the form of the hypotheses; and "form" in this respect is defined for linguistic representation. In addition, form in this sense is relevant where a simplicity metric is necessary in order to choose between hypotheses compatible with the data.

But it is perfectly reasonable to construe visual displays, such as graph curves, as if they were hypotheses, too. The same can be said for pictures. As Goodman points out: "Truth of a hypothesis after all is a matter of fit. . . . Goodness of fit takes a two-way adjustment—of theory to facts and of facts to theory. But such fitness . . .

is equally relevant for the aesthetic symbol. Truth and its aesthetic counterpart amount to appropriateness under different names."[14]

This point can be generalized to include other kinds of display. There is a legitimate sense in which one can ask how well a map or diagram or prototypical image fits a perceived or remembered scene and, particularly in the case of the prototype, how well the scene fits it. As Goodman's reference to truth suggests, there is a fundamental issue about the nature of the conditions on the fitness of representations generally: Is it something like accuracy to the facts of the matter or something more like usefulness or coherence? However, before standards are laid down on the goodness of fit or appropriateness generally, it will be helpful to consider what determines the special fitness of one type of representation as opposed to another in various circumstances.

The answer seems obvious. Which type of image is employed will depend upon the task at hand. A prototype would be useless for picking out a face in a crowd; a photograph of the landscape may have only minimal value for finding one's way home. But is there an internal correlate to these tasks? That is, a working assumption of cognitivism is that an account of cognitive tasks can be given in terms of a theory of relations among mental symbols. It should, therefore, be possible to give such an account for a cognitivist theory of mental imagery.

In a general sense, such an account is ready to hand. It would consist in defining a set of diverse operations, some of which are characteristic of images of a certain kind, while others apply to other kinds. The fact that I rotate it rather than scan it, for example, may distinguish a model from a map, independent of any reference to the set of things modeled or the particular region mapped. This sort of process account is consistent with a generally functionalist view of the identity of images. At least one basis for distinguishing modes of imagery will be in terms of the extent and manner to which they are isomorphic to their putative objects, that is, in terms of the degree and kind of nomic similarity they exhibit. However, the process account goes further and seeks to define type identity conditions in terms of different dynamic procedures. The assumption on which the analysis rests is that any task, say perceptual categorization, should be understood in terms of an operation, for example, prototype matching. This, in turn, will set limits on the kind of further interpretive procedures for which the image can be an object.

In a very real sense, this process account also fits closely with the relation between syntax and semantics envisioned by the computational model. According to that vision, as Haugeland puts it, "If you take care of the syntax, the semantics will take care of itself."[15] Specifically, in a formal system in which the tokens are symbols of mathematics or logic or language, the rules of the system will have the property that they are truth preserving. That is, if you start with a true expression and follow the rules, you will end up with a true expression. Truth is a semantic property, so here is one way a purely formal system can have a semantic interpretation.

Furthermore, there are two respects in which the symbol tokens have meaning as well as truth. In one sense, symbolic expressions can be said to be meaningful or meaningless, insofar as they are well formed. By itself, just given standard rules, $1 + 1 = 2$ makes sense; but $+ = 1\ 1\ 2$ does not. Second, there is a distinctive identity for a token like 2, which is the numeral 2 and which thus "means" the number 2.

This is, of course, a very narrow construal of *interpretation*, a wholly internal sense, born out of a computational model. A number of critics have argued that such a construal is not sufficient and perhaps not even necessary to assign content to expressions of beliefs, desires, and other states. I have argued that it is at least a necessary condition. After developing some important details of the theory, I want to consider the bearing of imagery on a crucial problem case in which this condition seems to conflict with how content would be assigned in light of contextual considerations. Clearly, a commitment to a narrow taxonomy of mental functions does not entail an outright rejection of the possibility of a broader construal of semantic properties. There are plenty of people, Fodor for instance, who profess to be realists about both representation and truth. In some cases, they are convinced that, ideally at least, taking care of mental syntax will facilitate semantics taking care of itself in a broad as well as a narrow sense.[16] I will argue that the link between the two, however it is forged, is stronger in a pluralistic theory that postulates roles for images.

However, a more fundamental problem must be addressed first: How do we take care of the syntax for nondiscursive images? Even to make the narrow type of interpretation a necessary condition on imagery, it must be possible to give some account of well-formedness for an icon and to say how the appropriateness or fittingness that is the counterpart to truth is preserved in operations on it. It is not enough to show that images preserve spatial relations to earn them a fully cognitive stature. An element of justification for the outcome of a spatially transformative routine, a normative or epistemic dimension, is also required.[17]

It is no surprise that this presents a challenge. The "interpretation" of an image, by which it is given a determinate content (with varying shades of determinacy), consists essentially in the manipulation and systematic modification of it. That is very different from an interpretation that is the conclusion of an inference. Nonetheless, the theoretical role analysis of narrow content can be usefully applied to nonpropositional images; and it does not collapse into a "merely" causal account. This is particularly clear insofar as one can show the plausibility of something like a visual syntax and semantics.

SYNTAX AND SEMANTICS
Images as Structured Configurations

In Fodor's words, "the formality condition does not preclude access to semantic relations when they are coextensive with formal ones, so long as the access is achieved, as it were, via the latter."[18] However, this is a more restrictive concession than it appears. In Fodor's philosophy of language, there must be a canonical form for representation, that is, one in which logical form is explicit; and this requires that the truth conditions of the representation be apparent in the relations among its components. In the first instance, this is because computation entails following rules: "What distinguishes what organisms do from what planets do is that a representation of the rules they follow constitutes one of the causal determinants of their behavior."[19] Since there is "no way of construing the notion that there might be a language in which truth is defined for icons instead of symbols; in which, i.e. 'formulae' of the system are true of what they resemble," it is argued that images must be conjoined with descriptions in the language of thought in order to play any role in cognition. The problem with this argument is its assumption that, because sentences cannot have an iconic canonical form, it follows that images can have no canonical form at all. This is the point I wish to deny.

My contention is that narrowly defined appropriateness conditions for visual forms, like truth conditions for linguistic formulae, can be canonically represented, so that appropriateness is definable in terms of formal features of the representational system. Indeed, I would further claim, this possibility is *required* in order to make sense of the larger claim expressed in Goodman's description of the process of mutual adjustment between hypothesis and data in the case of visual form. For the adjustment to work both ways, it must be recognized that the very form of the hypothesis imposes some constraints on the process; therefore, it cannot be simply a projection of the data. In regard to mental images, this means that their capacity for appropriateness as a visual semantic property must be mirrored in the visual equivalent of syntax, that is, the formal features by virtue of which the images are the objects of formal procedures. Since, as Fodor notes, "we don't know what semantic properties there are,"[20] it remains an open possibility that nonpropositional representations could enter into symbolic relations that satisfy the appropriateness conditions canonically represented in standardized forms.

The primary problem with the possibility of an iconic canon is that icons articulate no discrete subject-predicate relations, contain much irrelevant information, and embody no explicit logical structure. Hence, there is supposed to be no well-defined pictorial grammar or vocabulary and no obvious rules of representation.

But the fact that pictures lack syntactical features of the same sort as linguistic representation poses no real impediment to their formal disambiguation. Although it is often said that the continuous way in which pictures or other visual displays present information makes a visual syntax impossible, this simply is not so. The compositional character of pictures can in principle be exploited to get a basic set of features and operations that are fixed by hypothesis: lines, curves, rotation, projection, and so on. It has in fact often been claimed in psychology that perception and memory depend upon visual prototypes of the sort discussed in the previous chapter; and these might be construed as basic configurations in which prototypical structure corresponds to syntactic structure. Disambiguation and articulation would then depend on just what they depend on in the case of mental sentences, namely, an inherent canon of permissible shapes and transformations, derived from basic capacities. What is prototypical or canonical about any mental display, in that case, would not be its actual similarity to some object but rather its capacity to be similar by virtue of its formal organization. It would thus be the visual counterpart to a syntax that is canonical only formally and within a particular theory.[21]

Someone might object at this point that formalizing images destroys their analog character and, thus, undermines the distinctive contribution they might make to an account of cognition. I hope that the further discussion of prototypes and pictorial series below will assuage that concern, since they will be seen to depend on both analog processes and formal compositionality and to function in a way that is different from computation using sentences. However, I want to argue briefly that there are, in any case, some reasons to reject the assumption that treating images as structured, symbol-like configurations erodes entirely the contrast between them and sentences.

First, there are, as I have noted, several senses of the term *analog*. Goodman's conception of a dense symbol scheme, for example, is often contrasted with the view of a set of lawlike relations among physical values. But both assume continuity: syntactic and semantic on the one hand, mathematical on the other. The kind of compositionality I envision here—one that depends upon relations among exemplars of select standard analog states—is not inconsistent with that assumption. It is simply a theoretical apparatus for understanding how pictures or other displays can be employed in a predictable way in recognition and other tasks that call for judgments of similarity. In effect, I am proposing, for the sake of explanation, a formalization of the part-whole relation that is essential to the way pictures work. There are two points at which that relation is important. One is in the analog representations (or, if that seems to beg the question, in the constituents of analog processes). The other is in the analog processes themselves.

In the first instance, the fact that images are composed of parts that represent parts of the entire object represented does not undermine the employment of images in processes that depend upon their holistic, continuous character. Rotation and scanning are such processes; but they presuppose rigidity and regionality as constraints that serve to identify part-whole relations and keep them constant. In a rudimentary way, this illustrates how the explanation of behavior in terms of analog processes, in some cases, needs to assume a regimented model of composition.

One might object that the process itself does not have parts. At best it has states that are related as cumulative stages, indefinitely divisible. But that is sufficient: any selected stage will be describable (say in mathematical or probabilistic terms) in relation to any other. Further, the important capacity to identify *approximate* outcomes and degrees of similarity is preserved. The point of introducing the notion of formalizable combinations of states is then to make clear that, despite their describability in nomological terms, analog processes can be implemented in a variety of systematically related and predictable ways. Thus they can explain, in some cases, both the plasticity and the intelligence of behavior.

Second, not only are there intuitively different modes of analogness (for example, thermometers and photographs), there is, as I have noted, a continuum of representational types. As Robert Schwartz has argued, in some cases (for example, a three-term series of musical notes or a chess board), the analog-digital distinction cannot be clearly made. But the fact that there are similarities and overlapping near the middle of the spectrum does not eradicate differences toward the ends.[22] Ned Block and John Haugeland have argued that admitting nondiscursive images into cognitive psychology poses a challenge to its traditional ideology (though they appear to differ over the value such images might have).[23] I agree with that point, but hold that the challenge does not depend on treating the images as nonsymbolic. Moreover, it is not only traditional cognitivism that must rethink its ideological commitments in the face of symbol diversity. What might be called radical biologism will have to temper any tendency toward wholesale antisymbolism in its research program, if there are analog representations that are formal in nature. But these changes should not be seen as retreats from definite commitments so much as steps toward a more well-defined reconciliation and cooperation. And that is surely to the good.

Before proceeding to a fuller account, I want to take note of a potential problem that will initially appear technical in nature. However, the way it is ultimately resolved will bear on the larger commitments of the theory to a semantics for psychology.

Insofar as the status of an image depends, as I have suggested it does, on the theoretical network in which it occurs, one might ask: In what sense are identity conditions for it determined by its *intrinsic* organization? The answer is, in part, that the notion of intrinsic organization is an abstraction, in light of the fact that the formal features of images are functionally defined, and their function depends on the precise semantic properties for which they must be relevant. The situation is exactly the same for sentential states. Suppose, for example, that two terms are identical in form but have different roles: "Her cape was torn at the hem"; "The schooner rounded the cape ahead of the storm." The possibility that immediately suggests itself is to treat the word *cape* as a term, the formal value of which depends on the sentence in which it occurs. However, some critics have suggested that this possibility trivializes the theory, since it implies that any difference in internal relation could constitute a difference in form.[24]

The answer to the objection is that trivialization can be avoided by imposing a relevance constraint. It is possible to set forth what may be called a *principle of semantic relevance* for defining formal identity: Not just any difference in sentence structure will be taken to change the functional identity of a word that occurs in it, but only one that reflects a difference in the overall relations the sentence in question bears to other sentences. By parity of reasoning, this principle can be applied to any form, syntactic or not, so long as the forms are relevant to some semantic features.

It follows from this, by the way, that representation will not be ubiquitous. While virtually everything has some organized arrangement of parts that, to a certain degree, will be apparent on inspection, not everything stands in visually symbolic relations to other things. The perceptible forms of ordinary objects are typically good or poor relative to a nonrepresentational function. Thus, their appropriateness is not, in that case, a semantic property.

Although it will be necessary to add one further and important piece of theoretical apparatus to spell out fully what I have in mind, I want to elaborate the notion of visually symbolic relations to avoid the charge of begging the question. In brief, such relations are productive or generative, not by logical inference, but by projection. Of course, there are an infinite number of lines of projection from any configuration to others; but I want to suggest that only some will be warranted under certain circumstances. Warranted projections are constrained by principles of probability.

In order to make this point, it is necessary to say more about the adaptation of schemas and prototypes and to give some further account of the processes in which they and other sorts of images play a role. I have suggested that the identity of the image can be determined in part by that role, insofar as that is conducive to attributing semantic properties to various stages in the process. That is not to say that the character of those properties can be specified independently of a theory of the relevant processes. It cannot. The principle of semantic relevance, in effect, calls for an evaluation of the relation of processes to the ends and overall functioning of the system in which they occur.

That point is doubly significant. First, such an evaluation is not simply a theoretical constraint. Cognitive psychology assumes that an agent's behavior can be understood as conforming to or deviating from norms of which he is able to take account. Both specifying and taking account of those norms are facilitated by the language of propositional attitudes. The point can be put even more strongly: Relations among something like propositional attitudes will be required to understand how a formal system works in a genuinely productive way and how it develops toward greater efficacy.[25]

Second, the ends in terms of which processes are assessed need not consist in the drawing of conclusions. Sometimes they involve negotiating a visual environment successfully, where a successful outcome consists in recognition or perceptual categorization. And I am going to argue that those outcomes cannot be reduced to cases of justified perceptual beliefs. If I am right, then, to say that psychology needs a level of explanation for intelligent behavior that employs something *like* beliefs and if these processes are forms of intelligence, it will follow that an account of visual cognition in perception and memory has got to be expanded to include constructs at that level. In the long run, that will help to make sense of recent studies suggesting that appeals to a single type of norm, defined over beliefs and preferences, will not work.

The appeal to perception is explicit in contemporary theories of mental picturing: "Similar internal representations are posited to underlie all forms of visual experience (whether perceptual or imaginal). . . . At some point in the data processing stream, images and percepts have a common format."[26] Kosslyn argues that mental imagery must share common structures and processes with perception in the same modality. Besides its intuitive plausibility, there is empirical evidence to support that conclusion. For example, forming a visual image disrupts visual perception more than it disrupts auditory perception. However, the question may be asked, since the visual system already extracts features in some way from the retinal array, is another array necessary on which the same kind of operations are repeated, that is, are not mental images redundant?[27] This is a problem for a theory that tries to individuate mental states in terms of formal features adequate to tasks (such as map scanning) without sufficient specification of the nature of the processes that are supposed to carry out the task.

There is, to be sure, some evidence to suggest that the properties of images differ significantly from what subjects believe about perceived objects. According to one experiment, for example, the size (that is, the apparent angle subtended) at which images are spontaneously generated differs from that at which the objects are reported to be normally seen.[28] Thus, when subjects are asked to form images, they are apparently not simply recalling the typical perceived size of objects. And this is an important point, because it supports the argument that imagery cannot be understood in terms of beliefs about perception. But if images and percepts do share the same format, as Kosslyn suggests, to what are the differences attributable?

Suppose it is assumed that all visual cognition requires a syntactical element and that schematic and prototypical figures provide it. How would they work? Historically the notions of schema and prototype have played an important role in perceptual theory. Unfortunately, neither notion has been given a single clear definition. However, noting the imprecision with which the terms have been used, Julian Hochberg specifies a sense that is particularly useful, since it associates schemas and prototypes with the idea of canonical form: "The schema is the structure by which we encode (and can generate or reconstruct) more information than we can retain from individual items. . . . A *prototype* . . . or 'central schema' . . . [is] an underlying visual concept—a prototypical edge, corner, or bulge. . . . The prototypes can in turn serve as features by which the viewer can test and encode larger schemas. . . . Drawing an object in its canonical form . . . provides a prototype that the viewer can use for encoding and storing objects when he comes across them."[29]

The very idea that the prototype embodies canonical form carries with it the implication that the adaptation of schemas is a rule-governed process, since the canon constrains the further production of images, as well as object categorization. However, calling the process "rule-governed" is primarily meant to suggest that it operates under some constraints of probability.

The point can be clarified by a brief contrast with Gestalt psychology. It might be thought that invoking a concept of canonical form and related notions like mental schemas and isomorphism would mandate a theory in which whole configurations are perceived without the need for any sort of computational procedure.

Gestalt theory allocates a determinate role to salient organizational features in perception, to that extent eliminating any need for probabilistic inference. The theory postulates a higher-order mental apparatus that accounts for perceptual experience by virtue of its isomorphism to those organizational features. However, apart from details of neurophysiology, this isomorphism is of a different sort than that which defines contemporary theories of mental imagery. Primarily through the absence of any functional characterization of the implementation of rule-governed processes—which is the essence of computational theory—mental *gestalten* map in a more direct, determinate fashion onto perceivable whole configurations.

It can be argued, however, that Gestalt laws of organization can be explained at least in part in cognitivist terms and, specifically, that the minimum principle, according to which we see the simplest or most uniform possibility, can be explained by depth cues and a principle of probability.[30] I am suggesting, then, that schematization is a process that is not simply in accord with principles of probability of some sort; rather the principles "govern" the process through the causal effects of forms in which they are encoded. Second, the process does not consist in assigning values to descriptions of a stimulus array and then computing the probability of some combination of them. Instead, it involves constructing figures from basic spatially defined elements that are differentially available and fit together more or less well. Goodness of fit, in this case, is determined to some extent by the order in which features are selected. The possible combinations are limited by hypothesis; thus the value of any feature for a figural construction will depend partly on prior features already made available. The primary determinant of probability and fit, of course, will be the extent to which the structure can accommodate incoming stimuli. These considerations show that this is no simple template-matching model.

The possibility that a figural syntax and finite vocabulary might be explained by the production of visual counterparts to hypotheses has been proposed by others; and in particular, the encoding of visual information has sometimes been said to take more complex forms that consist in modifications of a prototype. To cite two well-known examples, Richard Gregory has argued for the notion of perceptual hypothesis, and Ernst Gombrich has postulated a principle of adapted stereotypes in picture perception as a special case of his view that all perception is essentially hypothetical. In support of his claim, Gregory cites a number of hypothesislike characteristics of perception, among which is the fact that perception can be ambiguous under fixed conditions and that what is seen is a function of the relative probabilities of the alternative objects that may be depicted by the figure: "This, surely, implies a repertoire of stored likely objects, the more likely being selected by the available data."[31]

As Elizabeth Anscombe has noted, Gregory must have in mind something like schematic sketches or models.[32] The problem then is that, if those are to count as hypotheses, we need a further account of the sense in which they can be well formed. That is, there is reason to think that the hypothesis and testing model of perception, which is the most plausible sort of account we have, employs visual standards or stereotypes. In that case, the need for a notion of form for hypotheses argues forcibly for a visual syntax.

Gombrich also gives no clear account of hypothesis generation; but there are two other problems that arise for his view that pose potentially even more serious trouble for a theory of this sort.

First, there is the question of how a set of stereotypes, as a kind of vocabulary of canonical forms, enters into the identities of *different* types of visual representation. How does the figural standard for a whale or a castle representation (to use Gombrich's examples) guide the production and recognition of a whale sketch as distinct from a whale portrait? So far, I have noted two ways of distinguishing diverse modes of imagery: (1) by the degree of resemblance, functional isomorphism, or nomic similarity images bear to their objects and (2) by their degree of discursiveness, meaning the extent to which either they depend on external interpretation or they include verbal markers of some kind. To that I have added the possibility of distinguishing them (3) by the kind of processes in which they can be employed or the tasks for which they are of value.

Let me reiterate that the point of distinguishing types of display for a theory of mental imagery is not so much to argue for multiple modes of visual cognition as it is to get clear about the kind of factors that serve to individuate whatever mode or modes have been proposed of late. Thus asking for an account of the relation of prototypes or canonical forms to diverse modes is a way of asking for further details of how they contribute to the identity of an image.

It is clear that standardized forms need not be components of all images in equally recognizable ways, as if additional features were simply added to line drawings to get more elaborate pictures. The point is rather that image construction employs features that are contained in standard forms and it shows the effects of their guidance in various ways. Diversity will result from the fact that there are several principles of approximation to the standard. As the cube-rotation and map-scanning experiments suggest and as Hochberg's analysis makes clear, we need some further account of the processes of active construction. Indeed, it is in conjunction with those processes that the best examples of the role of visual syntax arise, making the nature of it considerably more concrete. I turn to them shortly.

The concern for a process account also bears on the second problem for a theory of imagery as defined over a set of basic forms and operations. It will be recalled that, as part of the argument against a wholly propositional computer model, more recent prototype research was cited as an example of how concrete mental configurations could be employed in skills like perceptual categorization. The argument was extended to other concrete modes of cognition like paradigms that, by virtue of their holistic character, could serve to overcome the tendency of thought and perception toward a conservation of the status quo. But the charge of conservatism now returns to haunt the search for visual syntax too. The pictorial representation of perceptual objects, as much as descriptions of them, if governed by a system of set rules and a finite vocabulary, could be taken to retard seriously any development in it (even though it would not render the system utterly impervious to change). Merely having a semi-iconic system will not protect against conservatism.

This suggests that some further provision must be made for development within the system. Earlier I argued that a theory of development would be possible if the changes that occur can be understood in terms of their effect on the attribution of semantic properties to mental states. Those properties are, in the first instance, due to the nature of possible relations among symbols. Thus, we have a further reason to consider the kinds of processes in which these visual constructions might play a part, namely, to provide a basis for growth in the ability to adapt images to cognitive tasks.

VISUAL PROCESSES

In the discussion of the cognitive penetration of imagery, that is, the effects of knowledge and belief on images, I suggested that there is an obvious rejoinder to the attempt to use the need for a relatively stable architecture against the penetration of imagery, and that is to allow the effects to penetrate a series of images, keeping the basic imagistic vocabulary constant. I noted then that a fuller account of that possibility would be needed. We now see in what the basic terms and primitive operations would consist. But clearly not just any series of figures that show cognitive effects would thereby count as cognitive processes. More to the present point, not just any visual series would be semantic-property-preserving and thus pertinent to both the identity of a figure and such changes as would be permitted in the figural vocabulary over time. There are, in fact, certain specific conditions that the series must satisfy.

One condition is, of course, that there be systematic connections among the images in the series. Hochberg gives a good example of the dependency of a series on such connections in his analysis of how mental structures are necessarily implicated in the perception of motion pictures. The connections there are purely perceptual: Object constancy and the illusion of motion depend upon fitting each image in the series into a framework provided by schemas. Antedating the more explicitly computational models of Minsky and others, Hochberg's conception of the guidance, selection, and expectation that these structures set up is impressive. The important point is that this conception requires a *relation between representations*, namely, the series of images scanned sequentially and the schema that makes it coherent. This fact will add an interesting and important complexity to the analysis of mental imagery, where the relation (that is, both the schema and the series) will be entirely internal.

The significance of this point begins to emerge when we note that there can be principles governing the series of images that result in something more than visual continuity of objects and movements. Already there are constraints on the relations among images that must be respected to produce what might be called visual coherence: a poor alignment of objects in successive views can produce "accidental motion" that is difficult for the viewer to comprehend.[33] However, it is clear that the kind of intelligence manifested in constructing a visual series can depend upon principles of an even more demanding and subtle sort.

In 1845, the Swiss artist Rodolphe Töpffer noted: "There are two ways of writing stories, one in chapters, lines, and words, and that we call literature, or alternately by a succession of illustrations, and that we call the 'picture story.' . . . With its dual advantages of greater conciseness and greater clarity, the picture story, all things being equal, should squeeze out the other because it would address itself with greater liveliness to a greater number of minds."[34] But are there really two different ways to write stories? According to the descriptionalist argument, contrary to this claim, there is only one way to write a story, and that is to write it. Visual narrative must therefore be assimilated to verbal narrative if it is to address any minds at all; so the verbal must, in effect, consume the visual if the latter is to be a source of information. There was thus some prophetic irony in the fact that one of Töpffer's mentors, Thomas Rowlandson, entitled the amorous adventures of a character in his own visual narrative "Dr. Syntax in Search of the Picturesque."

I want to suggest that sometimes it is the picturesque that takes the initiative. That is, in some cases of visual narrative, any corresponding text is in fact subordinated to the pictures and not the other way around. Or at least we can say that the words are interpreted by the pictures as much as the pictures are interpreted by the words. In such cases, the relations among images, which may or may not be conventional, constitute a process that can contribute to fixing the reference or clarifying the content of any single image in the complex. I am not, of course, suggesting that propositional knowledge is not brought into play in accessing the information in a visual narrative sequence, but only that the contribution of the images remains unsullied by that fact.

The simplest example is the ordinary cartoon strip, but the history of art provides us with others that are far more complex. Take, for example, the depiction of Aeneas' escape from Troy, a scene depicted in various ways on friezes now in Rome.[35] While it is true that the story these pictures depict could be told without illustrations and that interpreting the full meaning of the visual narrative presupposes some knowledge of the story, that does not negate the fact that the relations among pictures in these series serve as visual interpretive mechanisms, in the sense that they display "rules" for guiding perception, by which the scene unfolds. Such a series defines a process in which the words are interpreted by the pictures as much as the pictures are interpreted by the words; and the rules for reading the sequence cannot be wholly derived from those of a discursive language.

But the crucial fact about these visual series is that, despite their uniqueness as works of art and, thus, as individual narratives, these friezes have something in common—not just a scene, but a visual story. What they show is that, just as the same story can be told verbally in different ways using the same basic vocabulary, so too can the same visual narrative be variously depicted, at least as a common theme. And this is a fact of considerable importance. Aside from a standard for the visual coherence of a series of images, there is a further condition that must be satisfied if we are to be able to describe it as rule governed in any sense. It is crucial that it be possible for different series of images to *represent the same content;* for it is only in that way that the same visual process type can be said to admit of multiple realizations. And that possibility is essential to the claim that analog processes exemplify the sort of flexibility to which I referred earlier that is supposed to be characteristic of higher-order cognition. It is that flexibility on which the very possibility of a rational standard, in terms of which there may be better or worse forms of cognition, is grounded. Apart from showing *that* analog processes can be intelligent without being reduced to computational procedures defined over propositions, the example of visual narrative suggests *how* they might be, that is, in what the intelligence might consist. It consists, in this case, in producing a coherent and effective visual narrative. However, I do not want to tread too heavily on the somewhat uncertain notion of narrativity in this regard. I take it as an illustration of the kind of sophisticated pictorial coherence that can go beyond the model of the jigsaw puzzle and help define a cognitive function for images.

On the face of it, then, one can say that the nature of visual hypothesis construction in the form of percepts and memory images can depend upon the nature of the relevant processes, the ends of which they serve (for example, motion depiction or visual narration). These will exemplify their own higher-order characteristics, visual semantic properties, as it were (for example, object continuity or a clean and dominant narrative line), to which the appropriateness of a given image is relativized. These depend upon the content of their components, narrowly defined.[36] Any changes in figural vocabulary that enhance the capacity to produce or preserve these properties are thus welcome, because the development of greater representational ability thereby becomes possible. Furthermore, while perceptual and visual memory processes may exploit the same format, the fact that there will now be a variety of ways they may do so means that imagery is not simply redundant to perception.

Nonetheless, there remains a gap in the account that needs to be filled. It appears in several ways. While the analysis shows how development for the sake of novelty could be admitted, it does not yet show under what conditions such changes could be expected to occur. Further, not enough has been said to justify the claim that the processes I have described, and the putative semantic properties that belong to them, could not be better understood in terms of beliefs about perception (for example, regarding motion) and preferences for descriptions of particular spatial arrangements. In effect, I have argued that there can be what Haugeland calls "cogency conditions" on visualization, insofar as a series of images can be visually coherent.[37] But the fact is that, on the prevalent view, the kind of coherence that is important for assessments of rationality or intelligence is coherence of belief, desire, and other propositional attitudes, and not simply that of a set of sentences or other symbols. Could it not be said, then, that a series of images is simply a more elaborate supplement to the propositionally expressive objects of belief and desire, the relations among which really do all the work in explaining behavior?

The answer is going to depend, initially at least, on the sense in which one is a realist about attitudes. For any view that takes the attitudes to *consist* in relations to internal representations (either as the single determinant of their semantic properties or as one of two factors, along with some other account of denotation), the nature of the attitudes should depend on the character of their constituent representations. If mental pictures are not simply propositions in disguise, then it is hard to account for them as constitutive of propositional attitudes.[38] For theories that identify attitudes with complex functional roles and that do not give internal representations such a central role, the question is open; it will depend on how distinctive sets of functional role interactions are categorized.

In the next two chapters I want to argue further for the view that the language of propositional attitudes, as it has come to be understood, is essentially a device for referring to relations among complex procedures; but some of the arguments for not treating images as objects of propositional attitudes will cut across that view and apply to attitude realism generally. I want to suggest that even if the language of attitudes is a shorthand device, it is a very useful device. The logic of belief and desire, as an overlay on a more complicated set of psychologically real computational procedures, is intuitively comprehensible. And intuitions are important in this area, where assumptions about assigning content to mental states and assessing their rationality have to be tested against what seems plausible regarding behavior. Therefore, it would be helpful and important to fit images into that level of explanation. That means, if attitudes are defined in terms of processes and some processes are nonpropositional, that we need an account of nonpropositional attitudes. Such an account would be expected, in any case, to complete the general syntax–semantics–process model. And it is needed to explain the conditions under which development and enhancement of the system could be expected to occur. It will also make clearer the ways in which images and perception can diverge. And, finally, an account of nonpropositional attitudes will shed light on some facts of human behavior and on what it takes to explain it. Like the corpulent figure of the Picturesque, who is reluctant simply to submit to Syntax, imagery may turn out to have its own standards of good behavior.

CHAPTER FIVE

Process and Content

The Case for Pictorial Attitudes

I was impelled to think. God, it was difficult! The
moving about of great secret trunks.
F. SCOTT FITZGERALD

It has been said that Rodin saw a particular figure intended for the lintel of the Gates of Hell as "contemplative"; that is, upon the lintel, "the figure was to contemplate the panorama of despair below."[1] In what must have been a moment fraught with complex emotion, Rodin is also said to have discovered that one figure on the Gates was an exact replica of the Adam of the Sistine ceiling, which he had sketched and admired forty years before, now rotated through an angle of ninety degrees.[2] Assuming that the contemplative figure of the Gates *is* the rotated Adam, one can argue that to say that Rodin saw the figure as contemplative is to say that he saw the earlier form as appropriate for his artistic purposes and, unconsciously exploiting perceptual information stored in memory, made various spatial manipulations of it. There is a sense, I want to say, in which this is a cognitive operation that anyone might be competent to perform mentally, albeit with substantially different degrees of aptitude. If there ever were an example of image rotation with a constructive purpose, this is surely it. However, what the example illustrates best is the way in which we are inclined to describe such unconscious activity in terms of its broader psychological impact: The rotation contributes to seeing the figure in a new way, namely as contemplative. Whatever else that means, it clearly implies that the transformed image is the object of certain beliefs, and the content of those beliefs depends, to some extent at least, on the procedures in which the symbols are employed.

On the face of it, this tendency to identify mental activity in terms of beliefs and other propositional attitudes is important. As Haugeland puts it: "Computational processes must not merely take account of semantically significant shapes, but do so in semantically appropriate ways. . . . What counts as a semantically significant shape, or indeed, a symbol, in any nontrivial sense . . . depends on an overall pattern or response which 'makes sense' about whatever domain is supposedly represented."[3] He is right. An account must thus be given of how mental images help make sense of some domain of representation.

One way to define "making sense" without having to develop a complete account of how mental images match up with the things in the world is to give a theory of the coherence of those images with the key components of cognition, namely, beliefs and desires. The semantic value of a given form, which is in fact what makes it a symbol, is largely a matter of the contribution it makes to that kind of coherence, however coherence is finally defined. Why, we might ask, does this term occur here or that shape there? Because, a reasonable answer would be, they are in some sense appropriate for the expression of my beliefs and desires. Thus, to have a complete theory of mental imagery, we must first be able to say something definite about the relation of images to propositional attitudes. For the starting point of cognitive theory, if not its final conclusion, has been the view that certain kinds of behavior must be understood in terms of the logic of belief and desire; it is into that logic that images must be shown to fit.

The question then is whether or not that fit should be understood to be the result of visual images working in tandem with mental descriptions, which are employed in belief-constituting processes. Having argued that visual images are structured configurations, the relations among which can be more or less cogent, I now want to claim that, in some cases at least, it will be necessary to construe these relations in terms of something *other* than belief.

In a certain respect, that amounts to reasserting the relative autonomy of imagery as a cognitive process. Insofar as various psychological processes can be taken to *constitute* propositional attitudes, claiming that there are nonpropositional attitudes becomes essentially a useful device for affirming that there are cognitive processes defined over something other than propositions. However, it is a device that carries a definite set of commitments with regard to the theory of mental representation. In the first instance, of course, there is the basic issue of whether a distinct category of pictorial processes is required; and that can be addressed even if the language of attitudes is taken only to be a useful manner of speaking. I want to go further and argue that the attribution of content to mental states implied by that language is essential to psychological explanation, and that is to embrace a realist construal of mental representation. The realism is of course qualified by the fact that it admits nonpropositional representation in analog processes. Nonetheless, for reasons I will try to make clear, I think it is a position that needs to be maintained.

As I have previously noted, one could adapt much of the argument for the formal individuation of mental images to a theory that dispenses with content in a broad sense, as in the syntactic theory of mind proposed by Stich.[4] Even so, there are reasons for giving a better account of the folk psychology of image and belief than we have gotten so far. Although I argue against this possibility, if belief-desire psychology proved to be wrong, the analysis of the role of images in it would make the case against content a lot clearer and could pave the way to an account integrating the formal counterpart of folk imagery with other kinds of putatively contentless representation.

A similar point can be made about an issue that arises for realist theories. On what Fodor calls "standard realism," though internal representations may be countenanced, the attitudes are not identified with various computational relations defined over them. Rather, attitudes are taken to be functional states of the organism.[5] On these versions of functional role semantics (FRS), the patterns of neural activity I have described as functioning like nonpropositional attitudes would have to be identified in some way that is prior to a specification of quasi-inferential processes applied to mental pictures. In principle that is compatible with the general line of argument here, so long as an account can be given of the relevant states of the organism and of the derivative relation of internal pictorial representations to them. There are, however, some prima facie reasons to think that the most plausible account of semantics with respect to images, and the one that fits most closely with the view I develop here, is some version of conceptual role semantics (CRS). Indeed, Block has argued that "none of the other semantic theories has a chance to explain the difference between the semantics of language-like and picture-like representations."[6] Unfortunately, there are some particular problems that plague CRS and FRS generally and suggest that, at least, they cannot stand alone. At bottom, the two most serious hurdles are difficulties in individuating the causal roles relevant to identifying attitudes and the underdetermination of the semantics of attitudes by functional roles. I discuss the first problem, and reject arguments that it is insurmountable, in the next chapter. A few points about the second are in order here.

One might try to address the underdetermination problem by combining functional roles with a second factor as the basis for denotational semantics. Usually the second factor is either causal or truth conditional. In chapter one I suggested that the truth-conditional approach seems initially more viable than the attempt to systematize actual causal relations, but it needs to be combined with a theory of internal representation to get a psychology at all. However, while I disparaged the causal approach earlier as the sole basis for a naturalistic psychology, I want to suggest now that it becomes more credible as the second component in a two-factored theory, more credible because the burden of giving a completely systematic account of causal relations is eased considerably by letting internal computational relations take care of the productivity of thought. There is little chance of correlating external causal relations with the multitude of logical relations into which beliefs can enter. There is a better chance of establishing a provisional set of causal categories, the effects of which are structured representations with computational potential.

As others have noted, the mapping of an inferential network onto functional roles to get attitudes requires a kind of idealization (to get around irrationality and false beliefs about the consequences of beliefs). But establishing a provisional set of (normal) causal categories (or truth conditions) requires idealization, too; and it is difficult to account for that without reverting to some theory of functional roles. The relevant categories will be generated by mechanisms, the functioning of which must be described. Simply invoking evolutionary theory in an a priori way will beg certain questions about how natural selection produces optimal function. However, adding a class of prototypical mental representations helps to ground the analysis and give the specification of the denotational factor some independent weight, because, although such perceptual prototypes are themselves part of a functional organization, their description is not laden with an antecedent theory of the *same* conceptual roles that the denotational factor is invoked to supplement.

What I have developed thus amounts to a specification of functional roles of images in terms of quasi-inferential relations. This approach allows me to exploit the concept of pictorial representation to get a much more systematic account than would otherwise be possible. I cite folk psychological examples to support the claim that the strategy is not merely an artifice. Its value lies in its applications, discussed in the following chapter.[7]

One need not venture too far beyond the standard analogy to perception on which pictorialism draws to adapt the propositional attitude model to mental images. Pictorialism assumes that images function like pictures in representing their objects. I propose that the analogy should be taken seriously. I therefore suggest that a model of picture perception provides the theoretical means by which to account for patterns of cogent imagery. Those patterns constitute nonpropositional attitudes that, by virtue of the analogy to picture perception, can be called "pictorial attitudes."

I will try to show how such patterns themselves can be represented in occurrent mental states. This possibility contributes to cognitive development; to that extent, imagination facilitates cognition.

REPRESENTATIONAL COMPETENCE

We have good evidence that there are basic pictures—ones which do not require any special training to understand—that we learn to see in the course of acquiring ordinary perceptual competence.[8] This is an interesting phenomenon, since presumably such basic pictures are not seen simply as objects but as representations of objects. The implication is that some of the conditions by which they function as pictures must be perceivable in them. If these pictures were seen merely by the application of the mental structures pertinent to perceiving what they represent, then, like birds pecking at Zeuxis' painted grapes, we would be tempted to treat them as their own content. The absence of training in this case implies that no special knowledge or inference is involved. Thus I want to argue that the perception of basic pictures depends upon a capacity for recognizing not just form but *relations* among form. The spatial relations depicted in the physical object are recognized through the application of mental structures, the relations among which are coherent to the perceiver. He sees them in the picture, having acquired a vocabulary of relations through experience. In that respect, they are like quoted speech: They have content, but they also *show* the conditions under which they function as representations. In effect they denote or depict the form of the representation itself. In Arthur Danto's words, they will amount to "form displaying itself as form."[9]

An objection to such forms is that they will thus show very little. Some supplementary semantical apparatus will be required in order to know what it would take to *satisfy* those conditions, that is, to know what the picture actually represents and whether it represents it well. To be sure, mental pictures will require interpretation at some point in the form of descriptions. However, I have argued that the notion of canonical form is a prerequisite for such interpretation. Further, the identity of such forms, basic though they are, is not limited to simple features, because they can enter into systematic functional relations with other pictorial forms.

The question that must be answered in that regard, however, is how best to understand those relations. The fact is that we do develop perceptual competence or, more generally, representational competence. The question is what sort of theoretical apparatus is necessary to explain that fact. This is the problem of cognitive development, and it intersects with the problem of distinguishing among modes of representation. Not only can representational competence advance through stages of development, it also comes in different kinds. There may be degrees of sophistication within each type; and some types may figure more prominently than others during various stages. Any theory of cognition that casts its net over a pluralistic population—including nonhuman animals, sophisticated computers, prelinguistic children, and language-using humans—must be able to distinguish modes of representational competence according to its general tenets.

There are two ways to differentiate levels of representational competence. One way is in terms of the sophistication of the rules and principles that are implemented by the system. The other way is in terms of the content of the representations that are characteristic of the system and the degree of coherence among them. This suggests that it should be possible to distinguish types of competence by identifying different sorts of rules and principles, on the one hand, and different modes of coherence, on the other.

Early on in the account of internal states, I argued that representational ability requires a kind of access to the relevant rules. Rule employment was defined as a matter of following the relevant rules consistently, rather than consciously consulting or being able to articulate them; but that possibility depends on there being access relations among states where formulae occur in which the rules are encoded. In that sense cognition should be understood as implementing rules rather than simply being in accord with them.

But that provides only the foundation for understanding the nature of coherence, the degree and content of which will, in one sense, determine kinds of representational competence. For coherence of a certain sort can be said to constitute the level of "comprehension" of what must be the case for truth or appropriateness conditions to be satisfied, or for content to be ascribed, at least as a necessary constraint. In that sense, what one needs is an account of access to the content of beliefs and to relations among them.

Representational competence, then, cannot consist just in a facility with operations defined over symbolic representations individuated formally. It seems reasonable to say that competence also requires that one use operations and procedures in a way that is generally *consistent* with one's beliefs, preferences, and desires. To be sure, inconsistencies can arise from problems in performance. But a characteristic tendency to misrepresent or contradict beliefs suggests an inadequate competence.

Of course, the ability to employ terms and procedures must overlap, in some way, with the generation and expression of a set of beliefs. According to the computational model I have been discussing, the psychological reality of propositional attitudes consists in a relation between a subject and a sentence, and that really is constituted out of a set of sentences. Any beliefs that you or I have are stored as sentences expressing propositions in the truth of which we believe; and those beliefs are manifested in various arguments and inferences we make using the sentences. This relational model is one way to identify content for mental representation, at least in a narrow internal sense, namely, in terms of its role in a larger conceptual and inferential framework.

For example, to say that Raskolnikov believes that Sonia is a saint is to say that Raskolnikov believes the sentence "Sonia is a saint" is true; and he makes inferences using it in conjunction with other sentences that result in his saying and doing certain things. And that is to say that Raskolnikov retrieves a formula from storage that encodes the information about Sonia, scans it, and then conjoins it with other bits of information in the performance of certain tasks.

On this relational model the implementation of computational procedures and a basic tendency toward belief coherence should coincide. It is thus a useful framework for accounting for representational competence with images. The examples considered earlier, of series of images in a visual narrative, fit naturally into it. Generally speaking, images in certain kinds of series can be understood to be expressive of an attitude because they constitute one. The pattern embodied in the series will exemplify what might be called, in the first instance, a visual preference. The tendency of the pattern to be repeated over time will mean that it is a characteristic mental feature, having the same kind of psychological status as a belief.

The significance of the comparison is this: When we attribute a belief to someone we imply that the believer typically employs certain modes of thought under certain conditions using particular sentence types. But the adaptation of images can also take forms that are typical of the perceiver; that is, imagery can reflect a tendency to use particular kinds of spatial or figural operations over time under some constraints of probability, a perceptual "style," if you will. The patterns of imagery are, in principle, susceptible to systematic explanation because they consist in projective relations among basic features and figures, according to probability of fit in two senses: formally, of parts to wholes; and substantively, that is, adequacy to novel stimuli, the performance of tasks, and the realization of goals. These patterns can vary from one person to another. In that respect they may be said to constitute visual preferences. Because they *are* patterns, they constitute the kind of mental states, the coherence of which is basic to the minimal rationality we presuppose in the explanation of behavior.

It is the importance of typicality, dispositions to think in certain ways, that makes the parallel with propositional attitudes something more than a procrustean effort to adapt a familiar model. Of course, embracing realism about attitudes is a manifestation of the commitment to contentful mental states; but it also reflects the fact that, while we are presently unable to specify precisely the relations that distinguish them, we recognize a variety of psychological causes and effects associated with the same contents. Further, we have a theory of how the types interact. I want to show that the theory extends to types defined over pictorial content. Thus, pictorialism is, or can be, the cognitive science counterpart to something more resourceful in explaining behavior than the introspectionist, associationist ancestry with which it is sometimes saddled.

The claim that there might be a variety of attitude types, in general, is not new. There are occasional references in philosophical psychology and epistemology to "perceptual attitudes" or a "visual stance," for example.[10] Paul Churchland in particular has argued that there are nonpropositional attitudes; he maintains specifically that the relational mode of attitude representation I have described, at least taken in a very general sense, is not limited to propositions expressed in a linguistic format.[11] He claims, for example, that there are also numerical attitudes (which take numbers rather than propositions as their objects), attitudes toward figurative solids, and what he calls "ubersatzenal" attitudes. Citing the work of Richard Gregory in perceptual psychology, Churchland maintains that our capacity for perceptual organization may be nonlinguistic, indeed, that linguistic categories of representation have been added to the capacity for perceptual organization primarily as an evolutionary coincidence.

Based upon this possibility, Churchland has extrapolated two awesome ideas. One is that consciousness itself may be nothing more and nothing less than a prelinguistic mode of internal perception, where "internal" presumably means "directed toward the central nervous system." The other idea is that, if it is true that language is only an evolutionary coincidence, then nothing prevents us from envisioning the further evolution of a *metamode* of representation in which can be expressed ubersatzenal attitudes. In this vision of the future, we will not simply have new beliefs about the nature of beliefs. Rather, we will have neuroscientific attitudes toward what we used to call "beliefs." And these new attitudes will presumably be expressed in a language of biology, although quaint ordinary folks may still lapse occasionally into the old-fashioned way of speaking.

Churchland's conclusions are, of course, eliminativist: Once it is seen that there is nothing unique about the semantic properties of propositional attitudes, then the appeal of clinging to a specifically propositional attitude psychology is diminished. I want to develop the idea that there may be special kinds of attitudes that are nonpropositional, but my aim is not elimination. Rather, it is a kind of theoretical reform, with an eye toward maintaining the centrality of the concept of mental representation in cognitive science. To justify the spawning of new attitudes we need to show that they can interact in principled ways and that they are irreducible to the propositional attitudes, of which we already have some understanding. If such justification is to be had, then we are bound to rethink our concept of representation rather than to get rid of it altogether.

I suggest, then, that there are "pictorial attitudes," which have as their content a certain perceptual organization or way of seeing the world. Like propositional attitudes, these carry the implication that a particular form, here given to visual features, is such that what it expresses can be appropriate to the object it represents.

Further, such attitudes exhibit other features very much like those characteristic of belief. Three such characteristics are notorious. First, beliefs are ascribed by a sentence in which another sentence is embedded: the assertion that "Marshall believes the Cardinals have won the game," contains the sentence "the Cardinals have won the game." Second, the two sentences need not share semantic properties: it may be true that Marshall believes something about the Cardinals that is, in fact, false. Third, a belief can be understood to be, in actuality, a complex psychological state defined by relations among sentential states that depend upon their logical form: Exactly what Marshall believes will depend on how he uses the sentence expressing his thought about the Cardinals in conjunction with other sentences.

Imagine, then, that rather than expressing her belief in conversation or writing, someone represents her attitude toward something she has seen by producing a picture. In that case, the three characteristics just noted are apparent: (1) the first image is effectively "embedded" in the second—that is, her perceptual experience or memory image is represented in the picture she produces; (2) the semantic properties may diverge—the picture could be appropriate to her perception but get the actual look of the scene all wrong; and (3) the picture is, in fact, the result of a series of perceptual or imagistic representations in which later stages are systematic variations on earlier ones, a series that may be said to actually constitute the attitude expressed in the view depicted.

What, precisely, the character of pictorial attitudes consists in is a matter that needs to be worked out in some detail. My concern here is merely to show that they fit the relational model and, in so doing, exhibit the generic properties of representational attitudes. Here the significance of a point I have stressed becomes clear. I have argued that pictorialism needs to pay more attention to the concept of pictorial representation that lies at its heart. In this context, the significance of that point is that the model of pictorial attitudes I have introduced, largely as a way of capturing the distinctiveness of pictorial processes, clearly depends on attributing pictorial properties to images. Or, to be more precise, it requires a process account of the properties relevant to the spectrum of images that display information in various ways.

I want to turn, then, to a discussion of certain properties that figure centrally in that regard, arguing first by way of analogy to nonmental pictures. Picturing, as it turns out, is a very subtle notion that allows for the recognition of representational content precisely in and through formal properties. This is so at least in the sense that the determination of content derives from an interpretive process that is dependent on those properties. The analogy thus sheds light on the nature of formalism and access in imagery. Consideration of it will set the stage for a further argument for the psychological value of pictorial attitudes.

First, however, I want to motivate the development of the analysis by showing that it is one we need to undertake. My argument consists in an extension of the claim that mental sentences will not suffice to account for all intelligent behavior. The corollary point needs to be established that explanations given solely in terms of propositional attitudes will, in some cases, be inadequate as well. I begin with anecdotal evidence, but drawn intentionally from a special source. Such evidence is entirely relevant because folk psychology, as it is called, has lately become fair game for philosophers of cognitive science. The issue of interest is whether cognitive science should preserve the central elements of folk psychology. It ought to be important, therefore, to know what those elements are.

Consider, first, Proust's observation that "when studying faces, we measure them, but as painters, not as surveyors."[12] Thus, at one time, a face may appear thin and gray, at another, smooth and glassy, at a third, waxy and fluid. These are arguably perceptible properties, and the point they illustrate is this: While we can simultaneously *believe* that each set applies to the same face, we cannot *see* them all in it at one and the same time. Thus seeing the face as having those properties cannot be a matter of simply believing that they are there. Nonetheless seeing the face as having them is to adopt an attitude, the content of which determines to a certain extent the logic of beliefs and desires that ensues.

In this respect, Proust's example approximates the infamous

duck-rabbit image, a perceptual phenomenon that cannot be explained in terms of a vacillation between two conflicting beliefs. I can hold, without any inconsistency whatsoever, both the belief that the image represents a rabbit and the belief that it represents a duck; but I cannot see the image as both a duck and a rabbit simultaneously, as I should be able to do if seeing it as one or the other were simply identical to believing that it is an image of one or the other. Seeing *x* as *y* in this way is *analogous* to believing that *x* is *y*, in terms of its status in a psychological theory; but the one is not reducible to the other.

I think we recognize something of our common psychological heritage in this matter when Proust writes that seeing the same face as thin and gray or smooth and glassy produces different beliefs and desires and, as a result, different behavior, although the seeings are not equivalent to the beliefs and desires. When one looks at the repository of folk wisdom that literary examples supply, it becomes apparent that while human behavior is of course explained in terms of propositional attitudes, it is often explained in terms of nonpropositional attitudes as well.

The need for these attitudes can be further demonstrated by considering their role in the development of representational competence. There is reason to think that learning affects perception essentially by reordering relations among modes of representation. And that reordering is not always simply a change in beliefs. For example, if I say that, at a certain point in *Pride and Prejudice*, Darcy sees Elizabeth as radiant and glowing, I do not mean that he believes that she literally radiates and glows. I also do not just mean that he believes that she is radiant and glowing in a metaphorical sense; because then I must be able to relate the metaphor to some of Darcy's beliefs about her literal appearance. The problem with that is that it is tantamount to saying that, in seeing Elizabeth as he does, Darcy forms a belief about his *own* perceptual experience; in descriptionalist terms, he tacitly exploits knowledge about perception. But according to Jane Austen's insightful psychology, it is due precisely to Darcy's pride and Elizabeth's prejudice that the character of their own perceptual experience and their own modes of imagery are quite invisible to them. They must learn, through almost heroic mental effort, to relate the qualitative and representational properties of visual perception to beliefs about perception. Failure to learn this brand of practical reason, as literary history declares from the time of Homer on, can produce cognitive impotence with dire results.

It would be possible to argue that this is only a special case of belief revision. These characters, archetypal folks as it were, come to hold new beliefs about certain antecedent perceptual beliefs, namely, that they are false or based on faulty inference. However, aside from the incredible density of theory-ladenness that this analysis would impose on all perception, and aside from the fact that there is evidence that people perceive and imagine things sometimes in ways about which they could not possibly have formed perceptual beliefs, this reduction would miss the force of the example. The point is that Darcy does *not* come to believe that Elizabeth has certain properties; rather he comes to see them as characteristic of her, as the object of his perception. His seeing her thus may require that he believe (perhaps unconsciously) that she is thus; but it is implausible to think that the change in the content of his perception simply consists in either a change in beliefs or in bringing a percept or visual image of her under different descriptions.[13]

These examples suggest a prima facie motivation for developing an alternative account. I suggest that the reordering of representations they seem to require must include changes in relations among nonpropositional images as well as among mental descriptions; and those changes involve dynamic processes that, in effect, constitute new attitudes. For a clue to how that could work, an understanding of pictorial representation is required.

PICTURE PERCEPTION AND MENTAL IMAGERY

Defining representational functions in cognitive science often begins with a metaphor; however, exploring the model it may suggest can provide a conception of functional equivalence, and that, in turn, can lead to the development of an account of logical features and processes that distinguish the function. It is often said that imagery is like perception in some way, and that images are like pictures. The implication is that having an image of something is like seeing that thing by means of a pictorial representation of it. But invoking these analogies is only justified if a legitimate and adequate conception of pictorial representation is presupposed by them. Pictures can only be understood to serve their representational function as objects of perception, that is, by virtue of their perceived properties. Therefore, it is appropriate to develop an account of access to the distinctive features of images in cognition, and thus of representational competence, by an analysis of some functional equivalence to the process of picture perception. If having an image of Mt. Saint Victoire is like seeing the mountain by means of a pictorial representation of it, then some account of access to the picture itself must be given. I want to argue that picture perception exhibits certain logical features, and those features can be used to explicate the role of imagery in cognition.[14]

There is, first of all, an interesting complexity in the perception of pictures, namely, that the recognition of them requires bringing to bear perceptual prototypes that are relevant to what the picture *represents*. This is not to say that no other mediating mental images are required that categorize the picture perceptually as an object, say as a drawing or painting. Indeed, the challenge of picture perception is to account for the fact that it would seem to require both. As Hochberg puts it: "There is no question but what pictures display the operation of mental structure; that is, of visual knowledge not given in the stimulus display, about the physical properties of objects and of their spatial relationships."[15] And mental structure is invoked specifically in the case of picture perception to explain content recognition. So, for example, a picture is seen as a cat reclining on the hearth by the application of a mental cat-schema to an array that embodies certain depth cues, as both a rule and a form of interpretation under a judgment of probability.

Of course, the attribution of content to a picture will require the use of knowledge, theory, and inference at some point. However, the representational function can also be seen to be the result, at least in part, of the organization of visual features. Indeed, the interpretation in the form of a description and judgment depends upon it. While not a sufficient condition for picture perception, identification of such features is at least a necessary condition.

Specifically, a picture is a two-dimensional array; thus, it has a dual perceptual status, insofar as it is seen as representing spatial relations in three dimensions. In that respect, it differs from a set of ordinary objects literally arranged in space. A painted canvas will be coincidentally a three-dimensional object, of course, but the depth represented on it does not consist in that. The surface of the painting is a plane containing two dimensional shapes and organizational cues. Yet it can represent depth.

The problem is that picture perception cannot be explained just by an account of the formal organization of the picture. Depth cues are notoriously ambiguous: The same set of cues can represent a variety of object configurations or scene arrangements. Evidence suggests that an unconscious inferential process is needed to see configurations as representing spatial relations. And that is precisely the mechanism I want to view as consisting in operations on spatial configurations, at least to a certain extent.

In that regard, the kind of formal operation on images postulated in recent experiments could in principle be applied to the identification of depth cues in pictures; that is, they may be thought of as general mechanisms at work in both perception and visual memory. In image rotation experiments, for example, some forms are depicted so that they are impossible to rotate in any way to match a standard form with a similar shape. Something like mental rotation can account for the identification of three-dimensional shape representation in two-dimensional pictures, that is, the development of a rational sequence of multiple transformations of the original array. So, for example, a hexagonal pattern is identified as a cube by "rotating" it, in the sense of altering systematically the array to see, in the relations among the transforms, what constraints the original pattern imposes upon them and thus, what sort of solid geometric configuration it could represent. Rotation experiments could thus be taken to elucidate the nature of mental structures and operations needed to account for picture perception.

It has, indeed, been shown experimentally that canonical form operates in perceptual processes, for example, in the fact that outline drawings provide information more quickly than photographs; and it may be argued that any picture can embody such form.[16] Since canonical form provides a mental schema with the character of a prototype, which can be used in perception in general, there is a sense in which seeing pictures can in turn affect perception. An artist is able to combine within a single view features that could not normally be seen together in order to permit optimal representation of form for perception and also to provide canons of execution that are unambiguous. Thus, departures from central perspective and from strict projective fidelity are utilized in the interest of representation.

I think it is clear, however, that postulating a set of possible mental operations alone will not suffice to account for how pictures are seen. Simply identifying a set of relevant operations would impose only minimal constraints on establishing representational content. Since it is possible to perform a variety of systematic transformations on a given figure, we must ask how the appropriate type of transformation is selected from the possible set. The crucial task is to determine what controls the implementation of one operation as opposed to another.

The problem of control is, of course, a large issue in artificial intelligence and cognitive psychology.[17] And a variety of proposals have been made concerning control, some of which I have discussed in considering the limits of descriptionalism. In addressing the nature of knowledge representation and the use of heuristics, the point was made that concrete, nonpropositional images would be of use in determining what operations are relevant for a given type of task. Since the task here is picture perception and the proposed operations are defined *over* imagelike perceptual structures, the point must be taken to mean that control is exercised in this case by preexisting patterns of perception, that is, by the characteristic ways the structures have been applied. The relevance of a given operation is, in that respect, relative to computational features of the system, that is, to the tendency to utilize certain patterns preferentially. This seems a rather natural way, in fact, to understand cognition: How one represents the world will be qualified initially by how one already tends to represent it. What one comes to believe will be guided by what one already believes. When the medium is imagistic and the task is picture perception, how one sees the picture will be guided by how pictures have been previously seen. To the extent that the relevant patterns are prior operations on visual configurations, a partial future control function is provided by nonpropositional attitudes.

There is then a question about the psychological reality of these attitudes. On the relational model, they would be largely dispositional, though the patterns of causal relations that instantiate them would have to be the result of actual mechanisms of inhibition and facilitation, encoded, as it were, by a natural selection process. However, as a further argument for including a notion of pictorial attitude in the theory, I will try to show that representational competence is enhanced when the capacity for representing the attitude itself is developed. And part of the point will be that, in that case, the exercise of control becomes less cumbersome and easier to understand in a way that mitigates the tendency to conservativism in regard to those attitudes. As an argument for pictorial attitude, the claim will be that there must, in principle, *be* something to represent in order to get these desirable results.

So far I have been considering the role of mental structures and processes in the perception of nonmental pictures. However, aside from extending further the analysis of points of contact between imagery and perception, the purpose was to establish an analog for the "perception" of mental pictures. Less metaphorically, the point was to get a model for an account of the incorporation of picturelike structures in cognitive processes. In that case, the conclusion to be drawn is that nonpropositional attitudes are required for images drawn from memory, too. Insofar as all images are quasi-perceptual and quasi-pictorial, picture perception is especially salient for understanding how they work. But it is now necessary to pursue a somewhat fuller understanding of the account of imagery in and of itself.

I want to emphasize first, however, that the analysis I have proposed is not circular. I am not simply claiming that picture perception can be understood by appeal to images and then giving an account of images by analogy to pictures. Three points should make clear why this is so.

First, I do not want to say that images drawn from memory, of the sort studied in recent experiments, are the mental structures that are implicated in pictorial representation. Rather, I am suggesting that something like schemas, prototypes, or canonical forms operate in both picture perception and memory imaging tasks. Independent evidence and arguments are given for that claim in each case, and the *explanas*—a set of standard configurations—is distinct from both of the *explanada*, so there is no circularity there. A similar point could be made about the scanning and rotating or projective operations by which the standards are utilized.

Second, insofar as picture perception *is* explained in terms of mental pictures (either because perceptual schemas are quasi-pictorial, even if not identical with memory images, or because memory images do, in some sense, affect picture perception), that need not be circular. That is, a general analogy to pictures does not amount to an explanation of imaging in terms of them. Consider, for comparison, the language of thought hypothesis. Language comprehension can be explained by reference to an internal language, the functions of which (for example, reference, inference, assertion, and so forth) are generally modeled on the external languages being explained. But the model functions are not invoked to account for the *comprehension* of the mental language. They serve to suggest processes that are constitutive of the mentalese that actually underwrites them. Similarly, modeling the functions of mental pictures on external picture perception is intended not to account for mental picture *perception* but rather to suggest how internal pictorial representation is constituted. Specified precisely, that then explains how the external model processes actually work. External pictures only suggest a model; the theory is articulated in terms of internal functions.

Third, the point becomes clear when certain details of the analogy are drawn out. I have said that there are two useful features of the picture perception model: (1) picture perception depends on a recognition of two-dimensional surface form, as well as three-dimensional content; and (2) the relation between the two is the result of operations applied under the influence of a control mechanism. That mechanism consists in a propensity to employ those operations in a certain way, as a product of past experience. It is a feature of the organization of the system.

Now, I claim that the extraction of information from memory images is similarly controlled and that the control function is encoded, as it were, in patterns of imagery. But again, it is not on those patterns that picture perception depends. Rather, it depends on perceptual propensities, that is, ways of accommodating incoming stimuli to stored schemas. Perceptual schemas are not on a par with images drawn from memory just because they are stored.

The more important point, however, is that the schemas or prototypes themselves need not be understood as being identified by some further controlled interpretive process. They are only quasi-pictorial, because *their* two-dimensional figural identities do not derive from scanning, rotating, and so on. Indeed, it is those figures that are transformed and so presupposed by the operations in question. Therefore, they are not actually like pictorial representations, and assigning a role to them in both picture perception and mental imagery does not introduce circularity.

Circularity aside, someone might still object that the analogy fails because there is in fact nothing comparable in imagery to the recognition of two-dimensional surface form. But here is one place where the extent of the analogy becomes especially apparent, for the counterpart to such form recognition is not internal recognition. It is simply the aptitude of the system to implement formal procedures to ends that depend on the particular arrangements of standard figures. Those, I have argued, are fundamental to understanding image routines.

In order to illustrate the general nature of pictorial attitude, it would be useful to have a concept that is as central and exemplary as the concept of belief is for propositional attitude. The most obvious candidate, given its recurrence in a variety of theories of imagery, would be the concept of *seeing-as*. For example, Kosslyn holds that images are the "retrieved encodings of how something appeared (the products of 'seeing as'))," in contrast to being the outcome of "descriptive information (such as the products of 'seeing that')."[18]

There is, of course, a well-known precedent for analyzing the concept of an image in terms of seeing-as. In the *Investigations*, Wittgenstein claims that "the concept 'I am now seeing it as . . .' is akin to 'I am now having this image'."[19] And the Wittgensteinian ancestry suggests a virtue of the concept for the attempt to use picture perception as a model for imaging: By using it, the complexity that pictures are both objects and representations of objects can be eliminated by analysis. For Wittgenstein, seeing X as Y can be understood to be an activity; it need not be mediated by an entity that represents Y. Ordinarily, seeing a photograph as a picture of something requires seeing the physical object as a medium.[20] In the case of mental images, a Wittgensteinian might say, there is no such object that is seen as a representation. As Hide Ishiguro puts it: "We are just left with activities of 'seeing as Y.' . . . There is no representational medium on which I correctly or incorrectly apply 'rules of projection' or which I see as depicting something else."[21]

This, of course, would be too high a price to pay for cognitive psychology to avoid the complexities of mental pictures. The "activities" envisioned by the Wittgensteinian approach will not be mental representational activities. In the context of cognitive science, however, the revival of the notion of seeing-as is simply a corollary of the claim that the capacity for mental representation entails representational competence to some degree, one way to make degree distinctions being in terms of the relations between the organism and its sentential states and mental images. It seems clear that *some* relation is required at any level of representation in order for there to *be* representation, since that means merely that a particular formal token is generated or retrieved and adapted to some cognitive task. The fact that something like that is presupposed by a representational function for a given set of formal symbols should make it uncontroversial to claim that representational competence must be defined with reference to propositional and pictorial attitudes. In this case, the logic of the analysis satisfies the intuition that mental representation occurs in the service of behavior governed by our beliefs, desires, and so on.

It might be argued, however, that trying to define pictorial attitude in general in terms of seeing-as, in conjunction with a theory that purports to respect the formality condition on the individuation of mental states, is self-defeating: It precludes an account of access to images in a way that depends upon exploiting their formal features.[22] To see *X* as *Y* is to bring it under some concept that entails describing or visualizing it as having certain properties *other* than the ones it does have. Thus, if I see a knife as a letter opener, I see it as having certain features that are not manifest in immediate perception. However, that fact in itself is unproblematic on the account I have suggested, since it can be taken to mean that the image is identified, in part, by means of its functioning together with other mental representations in some rule-governed process. It does not exclude the individuation of images formally or the exploitation of them by virtue of their formal features. If I see the knife as a letter opener, it does not follow that at the same time I cannot take note of its sharp edge and pointed tip. In fact, insofar as seeing-as is an appropriate candidate for a pictorial attitude, what it shows is that adhering to the formalism required for an account of mental representation, in the case of the image, brings with it precisely the complexities of picture perception.

My concern is, of course, with the unconscious functioning of the mental representation. In that case, to speak of "seeing the image" as a representation just means that it functions in the context of a representational process by virtue of the organization of its formal features. The organization will exhibit feature relations that, if they are standardized or paradigmatic for an image of that type, will exemplify rules of representation. To see the image as a representation in this sense means only that the role it plays in conjunction with other images depends upon coordinating them according to these rules. However, to speak in this way does make clear that the rules are a special sort, namely, those governing the relations among spatially defined figures and operations upon them. It provides the theoretical framework within which a set of operations like Kosslyn's scanning, zooming, resolving, and so on can be treated as part of an integrated procedure of a higher order that has some overall *point*. In this case, the point is to establish the content of a figure as a display—say, as a three-dimensional object with perceivable properties that only emerge *as* perceivable by applying the procedure to it: Out of shape, size, luminosity, resolution, and grain are produced vividness, clarity, depth, smoothness, dimensionality, and other properties of a more complex sort.

Further, it is necessary to have the theoretical means by which to entertain images *provisionally*, that is, without any prior commitment to their appropriateness for a task. In other words, there must be the possibility, in principle, for affirming the appropriateness of a form. Otherwise, any occurrent image would have the same epistemic status. Insofar as images function like visual hypotheses, there should be a way to account for the degree to which they are accepted. And one way is in terms of the extent to which they become characteristic of the person who has them.[23]

To recapitulate the central line of argument then: In order to give a theory of mental imagery, it is necessary to explain the logical relations among images in the cognitive processes in which they play a role. The ability to engage such processes constitutes a form of representational competence. That competence is demonstrated by the consistent adaptation of mental representations to cognitive tasks by virtue of their distinctive features; and consistency in that sense is determined by a coherence among the forms of mental representation when implementing rule-governed procedures. However, internal coherence can occur in a variety of ways; and the ways in which it occurs defines something like a set of beliefs, preferences, and so on for a representational system. Therefore, an account of representational competence must provide for attitudes of that sort in general, and in particular, the appropriateness of a mode of representation, as the object of some type of attitude, must be shown.

This argument has a number of important consequences. Since each of them requires elaboration, I will treat them separately in the following chapter. What is said there is a significant part of the argument for the pictorialist theory I have developed here. To the extent that a theory can be shown to have applications to various related problems and to shed light on them, its credibility is enhanced.

I will argue that we must avoid confusing characteristics of pictorial attitudes with properties of images in general in order to prevent a chauvinistic or species-specific theory of mental representation. Given the theory of imagery set forth, nonhuman animals have a capacity for mental representation that is not dissimilar to human capability but that need not be assimilated to the singular format of the computational model. This suggests that retaining attitudes in psychological theory is important.

Second, I want to argue for the general relevance of the theory to the question of the relation of mental states to objects and events external to the representational system. That is the point of major controversy in philosophical psychology, and analysis of the representational status of images will make some contribution to resolving it.

Finally, I want to consider the value of imagery for self-knowledge. The computational model of the psychological reality of beliefs holds that they consist in a relation between a subject and a mental sentence. Not enough attention has been paid to the nature of the subject in that respect. Some partial progress should come from understanding the nature of self-representation.

Taken together, these three matters will reveal the larger philosophical implications of the theory of mental imagery.

CHAPTER SIX

Imagery on the Bounds of Cognition

Arguments appear in surprising places. In a notorious work by Magritte, the words "Ceci n'est pas une pipe" are painted on the canvas beneath the image of a pipe. On the face of it, this painting illustrates the need to supply an image to establish the content of a thought; and in this case, the image is required to satisfy truth conditions as well. Here the sentence is, in fact, true only insofar as it describes the pipe with which it is copictured, for that is *not* a pipe but a picture of one. Of course, the sentence would still be true if what it referred to were the word *pipe* or a pipe description, but then the obvious point would be lost. In this context, it is primarily the relation between pictures of things and things themselves that is at issue. That the word *pipe* is not a pipe is not something that needs pointing out, since there is little danger that anyone would even look for a resemblance between the two.

However, there is a subtler point in the juxtaposition of words and object representation. The striking implication is that these are not just words either: They form the image of a description. And that parallel then suggests that the depicted syntactical form in those words will have a counterpart in the schematized visual form embedded in that pipe. There is, in other words, a kind of logical structure incorporated in the visual image, and it is depicted just as much as that in the imaged sentence. Thus, the picture seems to declare, there can be pictorial representation without imitation; and it employs formal properties in a way not dissimilar to that of a language. Viewed in stages, the spatial relations depicted in the painting taken as a whole exemplify the characteristics of a cognitive process.

In this picture, the words have virtually the status of quoted speech and the referential opacity that is a feature of it. One could not substitute other words that express the same thought without doing violence to Magritte's belief. And a similar point can be made about the figure of the pipe. Replacing it with another kind of pipe image will not preserve the characteristic way of seeing things embodied in the original. One could argue, therefore, that the opacity that is common to both components of the work confirms the claim that the pipe figure is on a representational par with the sentence. Both are expressive of attitudes, one propositional, the other pictorial. In that case, it is the compatibility of the attitudes, and not just the complementarity of the formal elements, that gives the work its coherence and the argument that it contains a kind of cogency. Magritte's other works bear that out: His pictures are consistent with a set of beliefs about picturing that could be extrapolated from the one I have imputed to this painting.

It is fortunate for pictorialism that pictures can be analyzed as essential parts of an argument for the pictorialist thesis itself. However, this example of self-affirmation is also useful for bringing out the significance of the imagery theory for three important topics: the attribution of content to mental states, the problem of individual and species differences, and the nature of self-knowledge. For the example involves a sophisticated kind of self-reference; and it is natural to wonder what sort of standard it sets. In its own way, each of the three topics I have mentioned circumscribes cognition. It is a test of a good theory to show that it has some application to matters that, as it were, define the domain. I want to show that the theory of mental imagery developed here applies in just that way.

CONTENT ATTRIBUTION

There is a sense in which the functional role of a neural representation can be construed as an aspect of its meaning.[1] If such a construal is legitimate, then what is called *syntax*, on the computational model, could be construed as part of functional semantics. In that case, the first-order properties relevant to the syntax of mental states would derive from neurophysiology. Thus, there will be one

sense at least in which it is true to say that "repeatable configurations of nervous activity" can be called an organism's "representation."[2] This analysis hints at the relevance of neurophysiological
investigation for cognitive science.

One question is how to characterize the relation between the
configurations of nervous activity that constitute a kind of low-level
syntax and the formal features that constitute functional semantic
properties. Another, more difficult question is how to identify the
relation between the functional semantics of the mind-brain and
the meaning we assign to external expressions of mental states.

In the first instance, I have suggested that neural configurations
be construed as functional configurations that can have the formal
properties of linguistic or pictorial constructions. The constructive
operations in either case I have described as basic imaging; and the
terminology is intended to leave the door open to the possibility of
a formalism not initially biased in favor of a certain type of discrete
mental notation.

These figures, whether wordlike or picturelike, are part of a network of patterns that can function computationally in higher-order
cognitive processes. How that can happen for sentences is uncontroversial; and I have tried to make a case for a similar understanding of pictorial processes. The case for pictorial attitudes has
essentially been an argument for the cogency of those processes and,
hence, for their cognitive status.

However, the parallel between beliefs and *views*, to coin a generic
term for pictorial attitudes, leaves open a substantive issue: Is it
necessary or even useful to continue to construe such mental states
as representations, the psychological reality of which consists in
the fact that they have content? Here, the notion of content is used
in a full-bodied sense that goes beyond internal relations alone, to
take account of the external conditions under which we should
attribute this belief or that view to a person, based upon what he
says and does.

I have argued that pictorialism needs a more formalized account
of relations among images themselves and among nonpropositional
images and sentences; and, invoking the apparatus of attitudes, that
is to ask for a principled inclusion of images in the psychology of
belief and desire. But that does not foreclose on the argument that
all the relations in question really obtain among states *like* beliefs,
desires, and views, but also different from them, as they are cur-
rently understood. The analysis could apply to a cognitive science

that retains the internal states, but bereft of their intentional content.

There is a sense, in fact, in which my analysis would seem to lend itself to that interpretation. I have said that some of the concerns voiced by critics of computational functionalism, specifically for the need to link mental representation to a larger context, could be assuaged, given a computational account of concrete, nonpropositional images. At the same time, however, I suggested early on that such images could be understood in terms more amenable to biology than proposition-based computation; and that is so, despite the fact that they constitute a level of theoretical abstraction that is in principle independent of any particular kind of biological process and applicable to many. Besides the grounding of the imaging function in neural configurations, that function, even at higher levels, is articulated in terms of physical values and spatial properties; and the specification of those values and properties could be supplied by the study of biological mechanisms described in a certain way, in terms of their relation to the environment. In that case, someone might argue, the purported intentionality of mental states is seriously attenuated, and the notion of the content of representation could go by the board in favor of a theory of sheer effective functioning, whether formalizable or not. Therefore, like the rationality of belief, the norms for visual thinking will have to be substantially reconstrued.

It may be that a reconstruction is in the offing; however, I want to argue that it does not entail the attenuation of the notions of content and representation. Without trying to adjudicate all the issues that have emerged in the recent explosion of interest in this topic, the scope of which extends well beyond the limits of these pages, I will make three points that, together, constitute an argument for a contentful cognitive science. (1) The evidence for images supports the distinction between a narrow and a wide sense of content for beliefs and, hence, for the need to relate them. That distinction, in turn, reinforces the case for nonpropositional attitudes. (2) Defining a role for images does help to establish a relation between narrow and wide content. (3) In so doing, it provides a resource for content attribution not heretofore exploited in theories of representation. To that extent, it weakens the claim that a systematic science that requires content attribution is impossible.

In recent years, the analysis of content for mental representation has often hearkened back to the traditional distinction between *de dicto* and *de re* beliefs. The general difference between de dicto and de re beliefs can best be brought out by illustration. For example, the belief that dead men tell no tales, as a fundamental tenet of piracy, can be taken in two ways: as a belief about dead men, or as a belief about "dead men." In the first case, the pirate's belief is about a state of affairs, to the effect that it obtains. In the second case, his belief is about a proposition, namely, that the assertion "dead men tell no tales" is true. The virtue of this ambiguity is that it permits us to give a psychological theory of how the content of beliefs can produce behavior, which is otherwise mysterious. The explanation is that de dicto beliefs are psychologically real, the relevant proposition being encoded neurally in a mental sentence; and the hope is that something like those sentences can be shown to correspond to de re beliefs as well, which are attributed on the basis of what pirates do and say regarding dead men and related states of affairs. The primary inspiration for this article of faith is the fact that both kinds of belief have semantic properties; in particular, both have truth conditions in some sense. The challenge is to show how the satisfaction of those conditions can be generally correlated.

Since the distinction between de dicto and de re beliefs is a traditional one with weighty credentials, it would be nice if it could be explicated in terms of the contemporary interest in the narrow and wide taxonomies of belief, or the semantics of attitudes identified with relations to sentences in the language of thought. But, I want to suggest, those distinctions can be made even if the de dicto–de re distinction is shown to collapse. The association of de dicto belief with mental dicta is a special application of the distinction, anyway, taken coincidentally to help explain it, rather than the other way around. The assumption that there are distinct de re beliefs that must be related to de dicto attitudes promotes a mistaken reductionist view. To say why requires a brief elaboration.

According to modern tradition, centered in the writings of Quine, attitudes can be analyzed in terms of the structure of sentences so as to distinguish those that express a relation to an object, person, or state of affairs from those that do not. Each kind of analyzed sentence includes a content sentence, but one of them lacks names or terms for particular individual things. While only those latter generalizations are notional (de dicto) in Quine's original sense, the moral of the analysis is more recently supposed to be that *both* types of analyzed attitudes include content sentences; and those sentences have counterparts that are psychologically real. That is, they can be assigned causal roles in behavioral explanation. Further, while only those analyzed sentences with names or terms for particular states of affairs are relational (de re) in their original sense, both types have semantic properties that can be specified in terms of what must obtain for them to be satisfied. Thus the de dicto–de re, notional-relational distinction gives way to a narrow-wide, form-content one that actually cuts across the original.

This adaptation of the original concern to a theory of mental representation can be illustrated as follows: Suppose that Ben believes the colleague who rejects his thesis to be misguided. It may be that he believes *that* some unidentified colleague is misguided. But it may also be that be believes this *of* some particular colleague. The first sense is de dicto, the second de re. But it can also be said that Ben believes that a certain colleague is misguided, giving a de dicto sense to that belief; and it can be said that, for example, Ben believes of his colleagues that the ones who reject his thesis are misguided, thus giving a de re reference to the other belief. The argument is then that the de dicto sense is essential to identify any belief, the question being how to relate to it whatever de re conditions it may have.

However, both Dennett and Stich have claimed that the difference between the two kinds of beliefs is unclear and that there is no distinctive category of de re beliefs. Dennett's argument is that notional attitudes are no less related to states of affairs in the world than are relational ones. What are purportedly de dicto beliefs are causally efficacious and have all sorts of ramifications for objects and persons other than the one who has them. Further, Dennett argues, the "notionality" of belief is bound to the expression of belief and to the network of causal relations of which it is a part. Since the identity of any belief is a matter not just of a relation to an object or set of attributes that is its cause but of a set of causes and effects, expressions of it have to be interpreted. It is the essential dependence of all belief attribution on interpretation that precludes the setting apart of a special de re set, the members of which are particularly well defined.

For his part, Stich claims that the kind of ambiguity that motivates the de dicto–de re distinction has just not been properly analyzed. He sees the ambiguity as a feature of content sentences rather than the beliefs defined over them; and he identifies what purport to be differences in kinds of belief as differences in the degree to which content similarity can be established between the beliefs of an attributor and those of the attributee. Whether to assign a de re or a de dicto interpretation to a description of the content of a belief thus depends on the context. And what this shows, Stich thinks, is the vagueness of belief content ascription, a vagueness that can only be overcome by giving up the quest for content in favor of identity conditions on the syntactically individuated sentences. For him the result of reinterpreting the ambiguity that led to the misguided de re–de dicto distinction becomes an argument for the formality condition as the centerpiece of cognitive science. That is a position that Dennett, of course, rejects.

I also want to argue, for different reasons, that the de dicto–de re distinction lends itself to abuse and that the ambiguity that has been taken to motivate it may not be exactly as it has been assumed to be. However, it is important to note that the conclusion that beliefs are psychologically real representations that may or may not have semantic properties is not dependent on locating an ambiguity in belief ascriptions and analyzing it into distinctive categories. Further, I want to argue, the need to ascribe those representational states on the basis of an interpretation does not necessarily deflate the pretensions of psychology to being a predictive science. In particular, the absence of a clear sense in which there is a *category* of attitudes about things in the world does not necessarily foreclose on an account of broadly defined semantic properties for attitudes at all.

The assumption to which I object in the discussion of de dicto and de re beliefs is that there is a basic sort of representational relation that is (1) referential, (2) reflected in a de re belief, and (3) explicable in terms of content sentences, which have the same psychological status as the content sentences of de dicto beliefs. It is the tendency to think of de re beliefs in terms of both their propositionally expressed content and their putative distinction from notional beliefs, which are essentially identified with *forms* of thought, that obscures the fact that basic attitudes might come in a variety of forms. The fact that we describe attitudes that represent the world as we take it to be gives the connection between description and representation a special but unjustified authority. The irony is that grounding propositional attitudes (whether they refer to particular things in the world or not) on relations to mental sentences actually opens up the possibility that other sorts of attitude (whether they refer or not) can be grounded on relations to other sorts of representations. Extrapolating from the notionality of some beliefs to an account of psychologically real representational forms at least has the virtue of leaving the door open to that.

I want to show, in that regard, that the argument that an image is not just a belief is borne out by the fact that, if there is anything like a narrow-wide distinction that applies to it, then what is recognized in an image is manifestly not what is believed. This point tends to be obscured by trying to ground the distinction on a fundamental de re sense of belief.

Suppose that "recognition as . . ." is a basic perceptual attitude directed toward a prototypical image. Whereas it may seem reasonable to assimilate perceptual attitudes to propositional ones when thinking of them in the de re sense, it is wholly unreasonable to think that "recognition," in a notional sense, is directed toward a mental linguistic entity. To translate the recognition of some object, say, a rose, into the "recognition that 'this is a rose' is true" would in that case be a pun.

The visual forms of notional attitudes might thus more aptly be called *de pictura* views, that is, mental representational states identifiable in terms of the semantic properties of pictures. In this case, the term *picture* generally designates not an especially sophisticated form of display but rather that content that is embedded in a display and expressed by it, as a sentence has propositional content that it expresses. Nonetheless, the reference to pictorial attitudes, I hope, will suggest how the account of nonpropositional attitudes should be expanded, namely, by going beyond basic states like recognition to attitudes that, given a more elaborate de pictura object, can contribute to advanced cognitive capacity. The autonomy of such attitudes becomes more apparent when it is made clear that what they preserve, as the companion to truth values, are pictorial values.

It is worth noting that there is a sense in which Stich's reconstruction can be applied to this approach to mental imagery and, in fact, can shed some light on it. The value of the initial attempt to distinguish de dicto from de re beliefs, for my purposes, lies in the fact that, whatever the precise location, source, and extent of the ambiguity, it can be analyzed in terms of the forms of representation. The pictorial counterpart to de dicto belief, a de pictura view, would be analyzed as what might be called a formal "notional array," associated most naturally with an exemplar or prototype that is not taken to refer to some one particular thing or other.[3] While not constituting a distinctive de re category, some pictorial attitudes *would* represent particular things. Ambiguity could thus arise because they, too, would depend on visual types as formal standards. More simply, it will sometimes be hard to tell if an image is of an individual or is an exemplar or stereotype for some perceptual category.

However, I do not share Stich's pessimism about disambiguating content sentences or other forms. I will argue in the next section that, once the account is extended to include images, the resources for identifying attitude contents are enhanced. In a certain respect that is so because some features of the context on which pictures and other displays depend will, as Haugeland puts it, "automatically" be associated with them. But that is due, I have suggested, to principles of (nonpropositional) computation rather than principles of association.

What, then, is the relation between the narrow and wide senses in which attitudes are defined? According to representational theory, propositional attitudes *supervene,* in some sense, on nonintentional states, either computational or neurophysiological. That is, if two individuals have different propositional attitudes, then there must be some difference in their nonintentional states as well. However, one primary objection to representational theories is that counterexamples seem to show that propositional attitudes are, in fact, not supervenient on nonintentional states. There are possible cases in which two individuals with identical physiological and computational constitutions have different propositional attitudes, because the identity of those attitudes depends on contextual considerations, either the way the world is or linguistic usage in a given community. So, in the classic example, two individuals with identical constitutions but living on different planets might refer to two completely different substances, H_2O and XYZ, when they say or think, "This is water."[4] In that case, according to the argument, they would have different thoughts, even though their mental representations were identical in every respect.

One reply to this argument, made by Fodor, for example, is to deny that the "narrow content" of attitudes, that is, the formal features necessary for the individuation of mental states, can be dependent upon context and thus to deny that individuals with identical nonintentional states can have divergent beliefs, narrowly construed.[5] The sentences expressing the beliefs could still have different truth conditions, broadly construed, if those are mediated by truth conditions on other sentences limited to terms for the relevant perceptual or phenomenal properties. Thus, using "This is water" to refer to H_2O in one place and XYZ in another constitutes the same narrow belief content, if it is identified within the representational system by its association with other sentential states incorporating only terms like "wet," "drinkable," and so on.

The problem in that regard is to specify the environmental features that produce the relevant states. But that problem becomes somewhat more tractable if the salience of the perceptual properties in question is said to derive from the set of prototypical images available to the perceiver, constructed from a vocabulary of features fixed by hypothesis. In that case, the task is not the impossible one of developing an exhaustive list of undeniably perceivable properties; rather it is to get the minimal set needed for generating others and, in any particular case, to define the others relative to the set. What constitutes the set will be an empirical question. Thus the fluidity and flat shininess of water in a liquid state could be properties of a prototypical set for liquids to which any particular instance of H_2O or XYZ could be more or less similar.[6]

Still, the deeper problem remains that there may be a divergence between perceptual beliefs construed narrowly and those construed broadly. The underlying concern is that behavior must be understood not just in terms of internal representation but in terms of the conventions, institutions, and practices that make up the community and context of linguistic usage. Faced with the possibility that the same internal states could occur in very different contexts, one proposal might be to divide up the labor and let psychology concentrate on what goes on inside.[7] That narrowing of focus need not produce a complete loss of contact with the social and linguistic context, because, after all, behavior is driven by an *understanding* of the principles and conditions that govern such a context. Understanding surely should fall within the domain of cognitive science; and I have made a case for the claim that the acquisition of it depends upon mental representation.

Yet therein may lie a paradox. Insofar as a thinker takes into consideration the contextual conditions in which his thoughts and those of others take place, his accounting and the application of it are apt to be "endemically vague," as Stich puts it. Stich would argue that the variability of practices involving reference and meaning is bound to overwhelm any attempt to attribute content to thought in a systematic way.[8] Indeed, the very psychology that seeks to regiment content attribution is itself the product of this vagueness, an attempt to define beliefs about beliefs based upon the kind of beliefs about beliefs that have been around for many generations. Those are beliefs about the content of beliefs.

To avoid this confusion, Stich argues, we can first recognize that we are not bound by it (since thinking we are is a self-perpetuating error); and second we can begin to think about the practice of belief attribution in other terms, namely, of identity conditions on syntactic mental forms. In that case, it is not necessary to attribute content to the mental states; their formal features alone will suffice to define the processes that produce intelligent behavior. That is, we can eliminate beliefs as contentful states from cognitive science. However, two counterarguments can be given, one of which lessens the motivation for this view, the other casting doubt on some of its presuppositions. Both turn on the possibility of nonpropositional attitudes.

Stich argues that attributions of belief depend upon establishing a dual relation: between a belief state and a sentence expressive of it; and between the attributor and the attributee.[9] This dual relation is the product of a judgment of *similarity* between the person ascribing the belief and the person to whom it is ascribed. Employing knowledge about his own beliefs and others like him, the attributor ascribes a belief to the attributee in the form of a sentence expressive of a belief that would be typical of the attributor in that particular situation. With this process comes vagueness and parochialism. Thus, Stich says, "to remove the indeterminacy, the cognitive scientist must adopt a taxonomy which is not sensitive to socio-linguistic setting or to the causal history of the terms the subject uses."[10]

Suppose, however, that our cognitive resources include images as well as beliefs. What I have suggested in the previous chapter is that there are reasons to think that the content ascribed to mental states in folk psychology is not always propositional. In that case, the first part of the dual relation described by Stich could be between a nonpropositional attitude and an image. Of course, when it comes to expressing states of mind, people are not image users to the extent that they are language users. Thus, the basis for attributing these states is not as obvious as it is for beliefs. Nonetheless, there is such a basis. Besides the production and recognition of actual pictures, there are all sorts of facial and bodily gestures, wincings and pointings; and there are certain kinds of voluntary and involuntary movements, for example, eye blinks, that have been correlated recently with internal processes.[11] There is, of course, no reason why the external mode of expression has to look exactly like the internal mode of representation, any more than natural language has to look like the language of thought. And, in any case, nonpropositional states can be expressed in words. In that case, the relevant relation that is established between a nonpropositional state and an image expressive of it involves the mental image of the attributor, a relation only mediated by external forms of expression.

The expected response to this possibility will be that now there will be two kinds of vagueness in psychology, each of which can be amplified by intersecting with the other. However, the first point I want to make in this respect is this: There is a natural sense in which the two forms of content attribution might actually work together to ground any particular interpretation. While ideological differences and other dissimilarities tend to subvert the neutrality and objectivity of a science of interpretation, the possibility of a second mode of representation not reducible to a system of beliefs can serve, at least, as a check on it. If we return to the case of Dr. P. for an illustration, we find an interesting visual counterpart to a central example discussed by Stich of the problems of belief attribution.[12] Here the question would be whether or not Dr. P. can actually recognize his brother, whether he can see the man as Paul. The temptation is to say that we cannot say, thus admitting a serious limit to the possibility of ascribing content to anyone's images. However, it seems to me we can say that, in fact, he does *not* recognize his brother, precisely because we can distinguish evidence for two modes of mental representation. The problem is overcome by our intuitive awareness that what Dr. P. says indicates that he holds the belief that this is Paul, despite the fact that what he does (failing to pick out pictures, explicitly listening for nonvisual cues, and so forth) shows that Paul's face is not the content of his perception. He can see the man, of course, but he does not see him as Paul.

The second point in regard to the possibility of a theory of mental representation concerns the judgment of similarity that is the key to content attribution. As a judgment, it presumably depends upon computation in some sense. That might consist in an inference employing mental sentences; but it might not. Evidence suggests that, in some cases, a similarity metric or a process of perceptual typing or a judgment of representativeness that does not conform to accepted standards of rationality is involved.[13] The argument against representational theory assumes that, to the extent this is so, one or both of two problems arise: Judgments of similarity will be inevitably unsystematic and indeterminate; and the very notion of content becomes obscure. However, defining a sense of content for images and developing a systematic analysis of the relations among them suggests that the conclusion is too hasty. These modes of representation may require imagelike structures; or the analysis of images could at least provide a model for an account of the systematic interaction of modes in judgments of similarity.

Developing an account of judgments of similarity that is both pluralistic and formal has two consequences, which reinforce the commitment to the concept of mental representation. I want to argue that, rather than promoting a tendency toward parochialism in psychology, ascribing attitudes within a pluralistic framework actually mitigates that tendency. It is, in fact, more likely that cognitive science will be unable to accommodate exotic folks and nonhuman animals if their thoughts, whatever form they take, are deprived of content. As an explanatory strategy, to dislocate the agent from his environment by eliminating from the theory of behavior any constructs requiring reference to external conditions is to discourage a recognition, in principle, of individual differences and variety among species.

Second, part of the real philosophical excitement stimulated by recent versions of eliminative materialism derives from their self-reflective character. They ask the philosophical psychologist to think about how he thinks about himself, and they suggest a way to do it. There is thus an appealing historical sense built into the eliminativist proposal, sometimes expressed in terms of a scientific revolution in progress. However, the possibility and desirability of radical change presupposes a theory of the mind's capacity to cognize about itself. This is not to say, of course, that any and all individual cognitive scientists must formulate theories of their own particular modes of cognition. And it does not entail self-reference in a sense that would automatically refute the eliminativist view. It does suggest that an account of the nature of one's knowledge of oneself, including how one formulates theories of knowledge and cognition, is essential to the enterprise. I want to suggest that one way to understand that capacity is in terms of the theory of mental imagery. As it turns out, this way depends upon the possibility of nonpropositional attitudes.

Each of these two consequences of a pluralistic account of representation—the accommodation of nonhuman beings and the enhancement of the possibility of self-knowledge—raises its own important questions. I will consider each in turn.

IMAGERY AND ANIMAL COGNITION

There is a long history of efforts to define a representational function for imagery primarily as a mode of imagination that may be accorded the status of metaphor or a constituent in metaphorical thinking (or, more generally, analogical thinking).[14] Sometimes this status seems to be derivative from the identity of imagery as an instance of seeing-as; but, of course, metaphoric comparisons are not the only type of analogy or of seeing-as. Part of the appeal of establishing the identity of the image in this way is that imagining has gained some acceptance as an attitude; thus there is a certain legitimacy to treating images as the objects of attitudes that at least are not obviously interdefinable with ascriptions of belief.[15] However, it is important to distinguish this particular role from others for which mental images may be necessary.

The idea that access to mental images is quasi-perceptual (in a functional sense) suggests that, taken as formal tokens, they are in a certain respect only *entertained*, prior to incorporating them in some cognitive process. But this way of thinking gives rise to important errors, because it glosses over distinctions among modes of imagery. To some extent, the gloss is fostered by the fact that having an image is, indeed, not reducible to perceptual beliefs, and it is further suggested by the fact that there is a sense in which the role of imagery in perception and memory is like that of a hypothesis. It does not follow, however, that the role reduces to any of the various ways imagining has been said to occur: pretending, supposing, thinking without asserting. The confusion has the consequence of undermining the possibility of levels of representational competence with respect to imagery, and thus, of discounting individual and species differences.

For example, Roger Scruton argues that imagery is a kind of reasoning in terms of appropriateness rather than in terms of truth. To have an image is like seeing X as Y, Scruton thinks, in the specific sense that it does not require asserting that X is Y. The image is a kind of unasserted thought, and the conditions for acceptance on such a thought are not truth conditions. This is so, to a large degree, because imagery falls within the rubric of imagination, and "the rationality of imagination is not the rationality of belief."[16]

There is, in fact, an advantage of treating imagery in terms of seeing-as in this way, namely, that it provides a general framework for construing some relations among images as rational. For example, Scruton describes how one's memories may acquire in old age or under psychoanalysis a coherent pattern that they did not formerly have. To that extent, his line of argument is a reasonable one. However, a problem arises when the capacity for imagery in this sense is taken to be language bound. While we can attribute beliefs to nonhuman animals, Scruton says, we cannot attribute any capacity for images to them: "Animals, who lack a language, and hence have only beliefs and no other kind of thought, cannot see aspects, just as they cannot form images."[17] The implication, one I wish to avoid, is that introducing the notion of seeing-as (to exemplify pictorial attitude) presupposes a sophisticated conceptual apparatus and a linguistic ability of a high level.

Of course, the argument that animals have beliefs but no linguistic ability begs a whole set of issues in cognitive psychology. To be sure, nonhuman animals may not speak. It does not follow that their beliefs do not occur in a linguistic medium of some kind. Second, there is no reason to assume that imaging always requires a high level of conceptual sophistication. Third, the concept of seeing-as is not identical to that of entertaining an unasserted thought; that is, the notion is not entailed merely by the fact that imagery is governed by appropriateness conditions for rational acceptance.

The implausibility of construing imagery as inevitably a sophisticated kind of seeing-as that involves linguistic ability can be shown by pointing out one of its consequences. Scruton argues that, given that nonlinguistic animals cannot form images, it follows that seeing-as cannot be implicated in ordinary perception. If it were, "the consequence must be that animals, who can have beliefs but no other kind of thought, cannot see," since they cannot see aspects.[18] But surely there are good reasons to think that something like seeing-as does operate in ordinary perception. One could argue, therefore, that the conclusion that, if perception involves seeing aspects, then animals cannot see amounts to a reductio ad absurdum of the concept of imagery that leads to it.

The problem here has two dimensions. One is an apparent confusion of the properties of occurrent symbol states with the features of processes in which they occur. Even if lower animals lack the capacity for imagination, that does not imply that they cannot form images, which are the constituents of more basic processes. This point seems obvious; but I stress it to bring out the significance of including propositional and nonpropositional attitudes in psychological theory: Identifying their distinctive features promotes rather than inhibits an account of the cognitive capacities of diverse species.

The second dimension of the problem is an extension of the first. I have argued previously that it is necessary to identify a variety of cognitive process *types*, to fully account for the development of representational competence. The consideration of animal cognition bears out that point. Representational competence as I have defined it admits of degrees, the level being determined partly by the capacity of the system to accommodate beliefs, preferences, and so on through the adaptation of symbols—words and images—to formal operations on them in mental processes. In that respect, it is attributable to nonhuman animals and children as well as language-using adults. However, I want to indicate more specifically how this is so.

In recent history, the animus against mental imagery as a mode of cognition has sometimes coincided with attempts to establish the existence of a mental linguistic code, which is presupposed by natural language acquisition, as well as by considered action and perception, and which is characteristic of any animal capable of intelligent behavior, speaker or not. While children and nonhuman animals are capable of cognition, they are incapable of using natural language. Thus, according to the argument, the medium for cognition must be another type of language. However, if there were a way to account for the use of images as pictures to represent the world in the performance of tasks, then the behavior of prelinguistic children and nonhuman animals that suggests cognition would not have to be based entirely upon mental representation in linguistic form.

The plausibility of the pictorialist thesis can be brought out by considering what would be required of animals in employing exclusively a mental language. Fodor says, for example: "The organism's choice of behavior is determined as a function of the preferences and probabilities assigned. . . . An infinity of distinct representations must belong to the system. . . . There is no upper bound to the complexity of the representation that may be required to specify the behavioral options available to the agent."[19] But it seems unlikely that all intelligent beings are endowed with an elaborate computational ability to such an extent. Therefore, there may be a tendency to misconstrue the abilities they do have if cognition is thought to be entirely propositional and inferential. Given that mental imagery is a mode of representation that is considerably less impoverished than Fodor and others have claimed, the demand for a sophisticated code capable of implementing an advanced decision theory in some form loses its force. While animals may have a capacity for systematic representation in the form of something like a language, I have tried to show that images can assume more of the representational burden than standard computational theories would allow.

Fodor's own recognition that there may be different levels and types of representation, which may vary in the degree of their explicitness or formality, that is, the relation between the formulae and the rules they follow, opens the door to the possibility that some mental representations may take a pictorial or imagistic form, depending on the nature of the task at hand. Indeed, there is one sense in which his theory requires nonpropositional representations. On the one hand, Fodor claims that the primitive vocabulary of the internal representational system is comparable in richness to the surface vocabulary of a natural language, and so, natural language predicates are not represented internally merely by definitions. But on the other hand he maintains that his view does not require that all (possible) concepts be innate. In part, the resolution comes from treating some concepts as "abbreviations" for others. But besides that, Fodor notes, much conceptual knowledge is organized around images, stereotypes, and exemplars. These need not be innate.

As Fodor notes, there is a problem with explaining, within the tenets of his system, how such nondiscursive representations are utilized: "The issues here are terribly difficult. How, for example, does one access an exemplar: If your concept of a dog is, in large part, a representation of a stereotypic dog, how do you go about determining what falls under the concept?"[20]

In the preceding chapters, I have tried to develop the framework within which that question might be answered. The framework is intended to be one which can accommodate some of the cognitive activities of both nonhuman and human animals at various stages of development. Some recent research on animal cognition can be interpreted as consistent with this proposal. For example, there is considerable evidence that some animals utilize mental maps in the performance of spatial tasks. The problem of access is clearly important in this light, and it is sometimes expressed in terms of representational competence in the general sense used here. For example, H. L. Roitblatt argues that mapping requires "that some function (in the mathematical sense) or process exists (neither of which need be a homunculus), which can interpret features of the representation as standing for particular features of the represented object or event."[21]

As Danto points out, setting up the relation of "standing for" as the criterion for representation in this case limits the model to a rather simple denotational semantics, which is not very remarkable when compared to a system capable of bearing truth values.[22] One could argue, however, that what is needed is an elaboration of the mapping process in a way that lends itself to the attribution of other semantic properties. What would lend weight to the claim that mapping is a representational ability in animals would be evidence that it is a process that can be performed well or poorly and that is specifically dependent upon the content of the map. There would, to that extent, be appropriateness conditions on it.

There are, in fact, other experiments that support just that possibility. For example, there is evidence that rats use extra-maze stimuli, like windows and sinks present in the room, as a kind of compass that specifies the proper orientation of the mental map relative to the environment.[23] In an enclosed radial arm maze, when distinctive stimuli are rotated 180° along the walls and ceiling of the enclosure and arms associated with previously unchosen stimuli are baited, the rats track the rotation and choose the correct arm anyway. If stimuli are transposed, that is, exchanged, they do not track it. One interpretation is that the rats treat the stimuli as a configuration, the relation of which to the map can be computed if rotated from the original. Under transposition, it is seen as a new configuration.

This ability to adapt a mental structure by reference to items stored in short-term memory bears a remarkable similarity to the relation of the hypothetical curve to data points discussed previously. Perhaps in an elementary form it anticipates something of the way, in general, in which mental images in humans are adapted to particular tasks. Specifically, in perception and action, images can be construed as functioning in animals at various levels of competence, like visual plans or hypotheses that contribute to those mental processes by virtue of their relation to disconfirmation.

One point of particular importance emerges from the interesting recent efforts, most notably by Herbert Terrace, to show that the representational abilities of nonhumans are nonlinguistic.[24] Lacking specific linguistic abilities like naming, the argument says, animals cannot name their own states of mind. Insofar as a capacity for self-awareness is a condition on consciousness, the implication is that the character of consciousness in nonhumans may be very different than our own. Whether or not nonhuman animals have *any* capacity to denote their inner states to themselves, it would be of interest to know how nonlinguistic self-knowledge could be generated. I turn, then, to a discussion of the way in which the analysis of imagery developed here lends itself naturally to such an account.

SELF-REPRESENTATION

It has sometimes been said that seeing pictures depends upon the possibility of attending simultaneously to the medium and to the object of representation; and, further, that this possibility accounts, in part, for the effectiveness of the picture and thus for our pleasure in seeing it, to the degree that the artist has exploited the feature. In certain respects, a similar possibility results from imposing the formality condition on mental pictures; and it would be an interesting point in favor of the theory if one could show that the imager could, himself, exploit the feature (though not necessarily consciously) for pleasure or for some related but more complicated end. Something like this seems to occur, one might say, in dreams, fantasies, and similar phenomena.[25]

It would be an interesting and complex task, beyond the scope of this treatise, to develop a complete and systematic theory of the role of imagery in those processes. However, I wish to focus on the way in which a conscious attention to one's images themselves can constitute a mode of cognition. In particular, I want to consider whether that attention can itself employ nonpropositional images, metarepresentations as it were, extending even further the cognitive function of that mode of representation.[26]

The possibility of representing, in some way, one's own characteristic representations is an important part of cognitive development, since it would facilitate either strengthening one's convictions and desires or revising them. There is, of course, a sense in which a thinker has access to the character of his own thoughts, simply as a concomitant of thinking them. That is in effect the kind of computational access discussed in the first chapter. The kind of access I now have in mind is of a higher order, in the sense that it depends upon the more basic sort but involves further operations. It is what might be called *reflective access*. Since propositional and nonpropositional attitudes can be very complex and their specification may require a lengthy conjunction of sentences, it would be useful to have a way of *representing* a propositional attitude without running through all the computational relations that characterize it. One means of acquiring access in this way is by entertaining belief-ascribing thoughts.

Thus, I can represent my belief simply by formulating a mental description of it: "I believe that diligence is the key to success." The occurrence of that sentential state does not, of course, *constitute* the belief; but it represents the belief in a form to which ready access is available. Such a belief-ascribing state has the useful telescopic effect of reducing a set of state relations within the system to a singular representation, implying the rest by relating the sentence to the subject who has it, namely, myself. In that case, the personal pronoun "I" can be thought of as a kind of collective name for a system of sentential states.

I want to pursue the larger significance of that symbolic function in a moment. First, however, the point to be established is that there can also be pictorial attitude representations in the form of an occurrent mental image, that is, an image which represents to me the way I actually tend to see aspects of the world. For it will turn out that there are important differences between the sentential and pictorial modes of attitude representation, precisely with regard to that telescopic effect. The difference shows something more of the value of imagery, in addition to its contribution to the cognitive functions earlier discussed.

Consider an extension of the analogy to picture perception, which was the original model for using images. Suppose that the context of picture perception is one in which the result is a physical reproduction (with some degree of accuracy) of the original picture. For example, an artist interested in illustration might rely upon the drawings of another artist to show him the forms of animal life in a part of the world he cannot visit; and he may also want to learn the other's technique, even his style. In that case, his aim is to represent the drawings and not just the objects that the drawings represent.

Something similar can occur mentally, in which case the two artists are actually one and the same. I can re-present pictorially a mental image of my own, toward which I bear a relation that exemplifies my attitude toward appearances. Call this a "view-attribution image." Such an image represents my view of a particular perceptual experience in the same way a belief-ascription sentence represents my belief about a particular set of facts, that is, formally, by reference to a mental representation that mediates my relation to the state of affairs described or depicted. "I believe that diligence is the key to success" represents my belief about diligence and about the truth of the form in which the belief is maintained. Similarly, an image can represent the object represented in the original image; and it also represents (without having to duplicate exactly) the form the image takes. The primary virtue of employing such a meta-image is that it allows the imager to picture the form his perceptual and visual memory judgments take; having that access provides him with the information he needs to try to integrate his perceptual judgments with his system of beliefs, desires, and so on.

In this case, like that of the belief-ascription sentence, the image represents an attitude: It exemplifies a relation between a subject and a mental image. However, there is an important difference: Unlike the belief-ascription sentence, the set of relations among mental images that actually define the attitude is itself explicitly exemplified in the image. A belief-sentence represents a subject-object relationship, but it does not identify any other sentential constituents named by the personal pronoun. However, a meta-image can display the component features from which the image has been constructed. The difference lies in the nature of mental pictures, which determines the possible kinds of relations among them. I shall try to indicate, in a general sense, how this might be so.

First, the pictorial attitude representation will exemplify the relation of the subject to a mental image by virtue of the "incorporation" of the first image in the second. It contains the first image by representing features by which the first is identified as an image of a certain sort and through which it represents something. In that regard, it exemplifies the fact that the image, toward the form of which I bear some attitude, is mine. It is a constituent of my mental representational activities. I have formed it; I can modify it and use it in various ways.

More importantly, the meta-image exemplifies further something of the relations in which the image stands to other images, insofar as it is constituted out of formal features that are said to have a representational identity. Where one image represents another as an image, there is an inherent representation of the fact of their serial relation: The picture contained must have been generated prior to the image that contains it. This is primarily a logical relation; that is, the constitution of the image representing the pictorial attitude is logically dependent upon their *being* a picture to which an attitude can be maintained; and the second image is constructed so as to represent elements of the original mode of representation. There is a sense in which this relation is also temporal, since a picture cannot be said to exist until after its components are in place.

There is, in that respect, a similarity between the representation of a pictorial attitude and *any* mental image: All images can be analyzed as displaying these relations to some other images, insofar as they are constructed from more basic detectable configurations. What distinguishes the meta-image from an ordinary image is that it is formulated for that purpose, namely, to preserve the features of an image specifically that identify it as a representation.

One way to depict pictorial attitudes, both for the sake of attributing them to others and to facilitate one's own cognitive development, is by means of an image that is especially *characteristic* of the images that fall under a certain type. The characteristic image can be regarded as something like a caricature that brings out and emphasizes the way images of the type in question exhibit perceptual assumptions and expectations in the patterns in which they occur. Hochberg provides a model for this sort of characterization. He says that an "artist is free to choose features so that each is close to its canonical form . . . and so that the pattern formed by the arrangement of features is also close to its canonical form, even though no face could ever be seen in this way from a single viewpoint"; and "if a local feature . . . is not disconfirmed by one of the other features, it will therefore evoke an 'expressive expectation' on the part of the observer."[27] In effect, such an image will be constituted by a dual form in which two aspects are combined. The relation between them is brought out by emphasizing their distinctive

features. There are the more or less schematic features that constitute the particular formal type, and there are features represented
as typical, for the person who has them, of the images used to individuate that type. To see an image as characteristic depends upon
recognizing the relation between these two aspects of it; and insofar
as it defines a pictorial attitude, the relation will be seen as appropriate. Thus, a further basis has been established for defining appropriateness conditions on such relations. In this case, the standard
of adequacy is twofold. It involves (a) the appropriateness of the
relation between the two forms, that is, the degree to which the
typical features facilitate recognition of the object or person in question; and (b) the coherence of the attitude with others in the system,
that is, among patterns of imagery and sentential states. And, one
might say, it is the possibility of such a standard that gives the
notion of reflective access its point. It provides the means of rein-
forcing the modes of representation that are characteristic of a person, on the one hand, or of changing them, on the other, if they are
seen as inappropriate on reflection.

The implication is that the limits of representation can be expanded by a kind of self-study, which may go on even though we
are unaware of it. This paradoxical claim must be a real possibility
if learning is to occur prior to the development of articulate consciousness, as it surely does in children and animals and, to a certain
extent, computers. To be explicit, what I am suggesting is that cognitive ability evolves by virtue of changes in the relations between
belief, preference, and the like, and the forms available for their
representation. Since those attitudes are essentially constituted of
rule-governed relations among formal representations, this means
that one condition on cognitive development (though not the only
one) is the recognition of new procedural applications of a representation, by virtue of its formal features and in relation to the features
of other sentential states or images.

This identification of a subject with the forms of representation
that are characteristic of him or her, I believe, is an important matter, but the significance of it might be overlooked. I suggested previously that insufficient attention has been paid to the implication
that a subject is a network of representational relations. Taken seriously, that would seem to mean that the concept of a person is,
at least in part, the concept of a network of relations of a certain
type. Further, it implies that personal identity is to some extent
determined by the kind of patterns that those relations tend to take

in any individual case. In that respect, we certainly want to know as much as possible about the nature of those relations, for it will be in terms of them that we think about ourselves.

The development of the details of these interesting implications is subject enough for another study. In this concluding chapter I have considered the possibility that a theory of mental imagery can elucidate a range of issues from animal cognition to artistic creation; such a theory provides for continuity among the many modes of intelligent behavior in the world of nature and artifact. In that regard, recognizing that the sentential states and mental images, which are the objects of attitudes de dicto and de pictura, constitute the person who has them has an important consequence: Those attitudes thereby become at the same time de re attitudes. That is so inasmuch as the object of the attitude is a *res*, an individual, namely, the person of whom they are constituents.[28] In the case of reflective access to explicit attitude representations, the character of that individual as a *res cogitans* once again becomes the object of mental representation. The hope of representational theory is that, insofar as what are represented are states of an individual who stands in certain relations to other individuals and objects in his world, the internal relations will converge on the external ones as reflective coherence develops over time. I am claiming that, given the specific function of images of preserving a variety of spatial relations found in the environment by way of isomorphism, combining them with beliefs as the object of reflection makes that convergence much more plausible. The view from Descartes's window of the *embodiment* and *formalization* of thinking things, with which we began, thus becomes more viable by crediting those things with a capacity for imagery as cognition. To articulate generally the features that a theory of mental imagery should have is to begin to transform that view into a science.

Notes

INTRODUCTION

1. René Descartes, *The Meditations*, trans. F. E. Sutcliffe (Harmondsworth: Penguin, 1968), "Second Meditation," p. 106.

2. Gilbert Ryle, *The Concept of Mind* (New York: Barnes and Noble, 1949), p. 19.

3. Ibid.

4. Zenon Pylyshyn, *Computation and Cognition: Toward a Foundation for Cognitive Science*, 2d ed. (Cambridge: MIT/Bradford, 1985), xiii–xiv.

5. John C. Yuille, "The Crisis in Theories of Mental Imagery," in *Imagery, Memory, and Cognition: Essays in Honor of Allan Paivio*, ed. J. Yuille (Hillsdale, N.J.: Lawrence Erlbaum, 1983), p. 264.

6. I draw the lines starkly around the competing views at the outset to establish the terms of the debate and to make clear that it raises issues about the very foundations of cognitive science. In saying that descriptionalism holds that all cognition requires a linguistic format, I do not mean that it rests its case *wholly* on an a priori argument. There are, of course, genuine empirical issues. However, methodological arguments are central to the debate, and they are taken to impose constraints that are essential to any good theory of cognition. In Pylyshyn's view, "the only real issue" is whether the imagery that is the subject of empirical study "ought to be viewed as governed by tacit knowledge" or not ("The Imagery Debate," in *Imagery*, ed. Ned Block [Cambridge: MIT/Bradford, 1981], p. 33). Pylyshyn thinks it should be and argues that only languagelike representations can be so governed; that is, only they admit of a systematic explanation of the use of knowledge in imagery rather than a mere description of its effects. Further, he thinks that the effects of knowledge on any nonsentential elements in the representational medium must be construed to be noncognitive on methodological grounds. Thus, as Block puts it, "the descriptionalists think that *all* mental representations are descriptional" (*Imagery*, p. 3, my emphasis).

CHAPTER 1. MINDING THE BRAIN

1. Charles Taylor, *The Explanation of Behavior* (London: Routledge and Paul, 1964), p. 6.

2. Ibid., p. 10.

3. Franz Brentano, *Psychologie vom empirischen Standpunkt*, 3d ed. 1925), vol. 1, bk. 2, ch. 1, p. 219. Cf. Dennett, *Brainstorms: Philosophical Essays on Mind and Psychology* (Cambridge: MIT/Bradford, 1981), p. 1. Statements regarding intentional phenomena do not have the same truth conditions as statements regarding nonintentional ones. Intentional sentences are *intensional* in the sense that they do not follow the rules of extensional, truth-functional logic, which is blind to intensional distinctions (since the intersubstitution of coextensive terms, regardless of their intensions, does not affect the truth value of the sentence in which they occur).

4. Hilary Putnam, "Psychological Predicates," in *Materialism and the Mind-Body Problem*, ed. David Rosenthal (Englewood Cliffs, N.J.: Prentice-Hall, 1971), p. 159.

5. Daniel C. Dennett, *Content and Consciousness* (London: Routledge and Kegan Paul, 1969), p. 45.

6. Cf. Stephen Stich, *From Folk Psychology to Cognitive Science* (Cambridge: MIT/Bradford, 1987), chap. 2; and Ned Block, "What Is Functionalism?" in *Readings in the Philosophy of Psychology*, vol. 1 (Cambridge: Harvard University Press, 1980), pp. 171–84.

7. Dennett, *Content and Consciousness*, p. 20.

8. That is to say, the logical state sense of *function* emerged as central in the evolution of the theory. So, for example, R. J. Nelson, "Mechanism, Functionalism, and the Identity Theory," identifies six uses of function: role-player, disposition, logical state, mathematical transformation, mathematical structure, behavior; *Journal of Philosophy* 73 (1976): 366. The "erstwhile functionalism" that he calls "mechanism" adopts the third use. There continues to be, of course, no singular notion of function (see Block, *Readings in the Philosophy of Psychology*, vol. 1). In particular, cognitive scientists dispute whether a functional description of a mental state must abstract away from all its physical properties. I argue below that it need not. The "core" sense of function is cited here as background for that argument.

9. Hilary Putnam, "The Mental Life of Some Machines," in *Intentionality, Minds, and Perception*, ed. H. Castaneda (Detroit: Wayne State University Press, 1967), p. 193.

10. Cf. U. T. Place, "Comments on Putnam's 'Psychological Predicates,'" in *Art, Mind, and Religion*, ed. W. H. Capitan and D. D. Merrill. See also Nelson, "Mechanism, Functionalism, and the Identity Theory," p. 371.

11. Block and Fodor, "What Psychological States Are Not," *Philosophical Review* 81 (1972): 169.

12. Cf. Paul Churchland, *Matter and Consciousness* (Cambridge: MIT, 1984), p. 56.

13. Jerry Fodor, "Methodological Solipsism Considered as a Research

Strategy in Cognitive Psychology," in Fodor, *Representations: Philosophical Essays on the Foundations of Cognitive Science* (Cambridge: MIT/Bradford, 1981), p. 227.

14. Ibid., p. 226.

15. Cf. John Searle, "Two Objections to Methodological Solipsism," p. 93, and Jerrold Katz, "Fodor's Guide to Cognitive Psychology," p. 85, both in *Behavioral and Brain Sciences* 3 (1980).

16. Georges Rey, "The Formal and the Opaque," *Behavioral and Brain Sciences* 3 (1980): 90. In this form, the claim is misleading, since it appears to assert a point about the genesis of the capacity to think. Rey's point is rather about the logical relation of the mental to the physical, given a materialist bias. Even so, it assumes that a functionalist theory is committed to identifying mental states in cognition by virtue of syntactic features. I cite it as an example of the theoretical significance of the formality condition for the philosophy of mind. However, it also shows a narrowing of focus inspired by excessive zeal for the computational model.

17. Pylyshyn, "Computational Models and Empirical Constraints," *Behavioral and Brain Sciences* 1 (1978): 93.

18. Georges Rey, "The Formal and the Opaque," p. 91.

19. Nelson Goodman, *The Languages of Art*, 2d ed. (Indianapolis: Hackett, 1976), p. 6.

20. Cf. Alvin Goldman, "A Causal Theory of Knowing," *Journal of Philosophy* 64 (1967): 355–72.

21. Fodor, *Representations*, p. 221.

22. John Haugeland, *Artificial Intelligence: The Very Idea* (Cambridge: MIT, 1985), pp. 25–28.

23. D. O. Hebb, *The Organization of Behavior* (New York: Wiley, 1949). See a useful discussion in Julian Hochberg, *Perception*, 2d ed. (Englewood Cliffs, N.J.: Prentice-Hall, 1978), pp. 90–93. The reference to patterns of neural activity will call to mind the more recent interest in connectionism. A number of researchers have claimed that perception and other modes of cognition can best be understood in terms of the activation of regions of the brain that are interconnected in a parallel architecture. On this model, representation is not local, but distributed; and it is said not to employ the manipulation of symbols or the application of rules. However, the conception of symbol and rule that is rejected is a restrictive one, derived from a linguistic model. I use the notions in the analysis of patterns of imagery because I want to argue for the usefulness of attributing content to cognitive processes. In general, the extent of parallel distributed processing in cognition is uncertain, and its theoretical implications are unclear. Despite their special properties, "distributed representations" would seem to involve *reference*; hence I want to argue that, even though they are widely distributed, they may prove to encode rules of some sort. These they "employ" by consistent implementation rather than consultation. Further, the

distribution of patterns in some cases would not foreclose on the need for local images and other nonpropositional structures altogether. Cf. David E. Rumelhart, James Mclelland, and the PDP Group, *Parallel Distributed Processing*, vol. 1 (Cambridge: MIT, 1986), chaps. 1 and 3; see also Patricia Churchland, *Neurophilosophy* (Cambridge: MIT, 1986), pp. 458–74; and Stephen Kosslyn and Gary Hatfield, "Representation without Symbol Systems," *Social Research* 51 (1984): 1019–45. The argument of Kosslyn and Hatfield that some cognitive processes can be identified as nonsymbolic representation does not imply that Kosslyn's theory of imagery should be understood in those terms.

24. This kind of access is discussed by Daniel Dennett in "Toward a Cognitive Theory of Consciousness," in *Brainstorms*, p. 151.

25. Fodor, "Methodological Solipsism," in *Representations*.

26. Stephen Stich, *From Folk Psychology to Cognitive Science*, p. 161. See also an earlier treatment by Stich in "Autonomous Psychology and the Belief-Desire Thesis," *The Monist* 61 (1978).

CHAPTER 2. THE LIMITS OF IMAGINATION

1. John R. Anderson, "Arguments Concerning Representations for Mental Imagery," *Psychological Review* 85 (1978): 249–77.

2. Pylyshyn, *Computation and Cognition*, chap. 7.

3. R. N. Shepard, "Form, Formation, and Transformation of Internal Representations," in *Contemporary Issues in Cognitive Psychology*, ed. R. Solso (Washington: Winston & Sons, 1973); Shepard, "The Mental Image," *American Psychologist* 33 (1978): 123–37.

4. S. M. Kosslyn, S. Pinker, G. E. Smith, and S. P. Schwartz, "On the Demystification of Mental Imagery," *Behavioral and Brain Sciences* 2 (1979): 535–48; reprinted in Block, *Imagery*, pp. 131–50. Cf. R. Brown and R. J. Herrnstein, "Icons and Images," in Block, *Imagery*, pp. 30–44.

5. Plato, *Protagoras* 331D, trans. W. K. Guthrie (Hammondsworth: Penguin, 1956). "There is a sense in which black resembles white, and hard soft, and so on with all other things that present the most contrary appearances." It might go some distance toward overcoming this objection to try to limit resemblance to perceptible properties. However, such a restriction would be arbitrary. What constitutes a manifest or perceptible property is unclear if it must be such that it precludes Plato's example of color. This shows the necessity of limiting resemblance to only those respects relevant to the picturing function; but if picturing itself is defined in terms of resemblance, the account is obviously circular. Resemblance must have an independent criterion if it is to serve as an account of pictorial representation. Cf. Nelson Goodman, *Languages of Art*, pp. 3–5, who notes also that resemblance is reflexive and picturing is not: An object resembles itself to the maximum degree but rarely represents itself.

6. Goodman, *Languages of Art*, p. 4.

7. R. N. Shepard and Lynn Cooper, *Mental Images and Their Transformation* (Cambridge: MIT, 1986), p. 14 and p. 102.

8. The example comes from Pylyshyn, "The Imagery Debate," in Block, *Imagery*, p. 152.

9. Both the reliance on the protomodel and the attempt to abstract from it can be found in Kosslyn, et al., "Demystification of Mental Imagery," pp. 131–50. Cf. Pylyshyn's reply, "Imagery Theory": "It is still only the protomodel that continues to carry the explanatory burden"; *Behavioral and Brain Sciences* 2 (1979): 562.

10. Pylyshyn, "The Imagery Debate," p. 167.

11. I. P. Howard, "Recognition and Knowledge of the Water-Level Principle," *Perception* 7 (1978): 151–60. Cf. Pylyshyn, "The Imagery Debate," p. 171.

12. That is, the effects "must" be explained in descriptionalist terms, not because a general pictorial model cannot accommodate them at all but because it does not do so sufficiently well. Further, the argument says, a properly developed theory will either be a type of descriptionalism or it will be one in which sentential states carry the explanatory burden. See note 6 in the introduction for references.

13. Cf. the interesting discussion in Robert Schwartz, "Imagery—There's More To It Than Meets the Eye," in Block, *Imagery*, pp. 109ff.

14. John Haugeland, "Semantic Engines," in *Mind Design*, ed. John Haugeland (Cambridge: MIT, 1982), p. 3.

15. Haugeland, "The Nature and Plausibility of Cognitivism," *Behavioral and Brain Sciences* 1 (1978): 215–60.

16. Haugeland's point is to show the presuppositions of a cognitivism based upon GOFAI: Good old-fashioned artificial intelligence. He questions the adequacy of this approach, proposing a holographic model as a plausible alternative for some cognitive processes. Regarding images of the sort studied by Shepard and Kosslyn, he suggests that they have real value for solving the frame problem, a point I discuss in a later section. However, he suggests that they can only be accommodated by a "segregation strategy," which assumes that cognition and imagery are entirely different and interact only via a cognitive input/output interface. See Haugeland, *Artificial Intelligence*, p. 228. Both the assumption that images are noncognitive and the problem of defining the nature of the interface make this solution vulnerable to serious criticism in terms I develop at length in later chapters.

17. Pylyshyn, *Computation and Cognition*, p. 201.

18. Goodman, *Languages of Art*, pp. 136ff.

19. Pylyshyn, "The Imagery Debate," in Block, *Imagery*, p. 218.

20. Block and Fodor, "What Psychological States Are Not," p. 162. David Lewis, "An Argument for the Identity Theory," in Rosenthal, *Materialism and the Mind-Body Problem*, p. 163, argues that a functional state is really

a functionally specified state that may be a brain state. The sense of psychological statements involves a specification of the causal roles of a state, "its syndrome of most typical causes and effects," and the sense of physical statements involves a detailed description of the state. Lewis argues against the demand for a universal correlation of contexts implying a single common brain state on the ground that there is a tacit relativity in one term of the identity statement, e.g., the denotation of "pain," which would be specified if the elliptical "brain state" were filled out. Cf. Bruce Aune, "Comments on Putnam's 'Psychological Predicates,'" in Capitan and Merrill, *Art, Mind, and Religion,* p. 51, who argues that functional state hypothesis is not inconsistent with the brain state hypothesis and cites Schlick's suggestion that concepts of mental states (as functional states) only capture formal features and not empirical content.

21. Jerry Fodor, *The Language of Thought* (New York: Crowell, 1975), p. 180.

22. Pylyshyn, *Computation and Cognition,* pp. 130ff.

23. Pylyshyn, "Computation and Cognition: Issues in the Foundations of Cognitive Science," *Behavioral and Brain Sciences* 3 (1980): 130.

24. Jerry Fodor, "The Mind-Body Problem," *Scientific American* 244 (1981): 123.

25. John Haugeland, "Psychology and Computational Architecture," *Behavioral and Brain Sciences* 3 (1980): 138.

26. Cf. Paul Churchland, "Plasticity: Conceptual and Neuronal": "Little or nothing is cognitively impenetrable save the functional features of cellular DNA"; *Behavioral and Brain Sciences* 3 (1980): 133. Cf. Steven Pinker, "Explanations in Theories of Language and of Imagery," *Behavioral and Brain Sciences* 3 (1980): 148.

27. Pylyshyn, "The Imagery Debate," p. 186.

28. Stephen Pinker, "Explanations in Theories of Language and of Imagery," *Behavioral and Brain Sciences* 3 (1980): 148.

29. I want to be clear about what is at issue in arguing for or against pictorial grammar. The important question, I am going to argue, is whether mental pictures or other displays can be part of a combinatorial system that is productive of semantic properties for propositional attitudes. It is, of course, controversial whether content and truth conditions on beliefs and desires derive from relations to syntactically defined mental representations. It may be that the semantic properties of attitudes derive from their functional roles, specified in terms of states of the organism. The semantic properties of an internal language have no special priority in that case; indeed, they may be said themselves to depend on the antecedent content of attitudes, notably the thinker's intentions. Therefore, lacking a linguistic structure does not necessarily deprive imagery of content and cognitive value, which could be ascribed on the model of functional role semantics.

Nonetheless, I am going to argue that images-as-displays are on a par with mental sentences, in that relations to images play an essential role in determining the content of attitudes. The analogy to sentences will require further argument, both in spelling out details and in rebuttal of the claim that pictures and analog processes cannot be analyzed in this way without destroying what is distinctive about them. I save that argument for later.

30. There has been considerable pressure from various quarters in recent years to displace propositional attitude psychology from its privileged position and, on some views, to eliminate it from cognitive science. My concern here could be expressed in a way that is independent of the outcome of that pressure by adding two qualifications. First, I will argue later that folk psychology includes mental images as pictures or other displays, as well as beliefs and desires. Images play a more substantive, integrated role than current theories suggest. We had better understand that role before we begin dispensing with psychological traditions. Second, even if a radical change is in the offing, there is at least as much reason to expect pluralism to endure as not. If it does, the need to understand relations among modes of cognition will remain. For example, if β-states replace beliefs (identified, as some would have it, by syntactic form without content), then ι-states may replace images. The relations among β- and ι-states will have to be elucidated. However, I will argue near the end of this study that a positive theory of the contentful character of mental imagery relieves some of the eliminativist pressure.

CHAPTER 3. THE POVERTY OF DESCRIPTIONALISM

1. Oliver Sacks, "The Man Who Mistook His Wife for a Hat," in *The Man Who Mistook His Wife for a Hat* (New York: Harper & Row, 1985), p. 13.

2. Ibid., p. 13.

3. S. Kosslyn, "The Medium and the Message in Mental Imagery," in Block, *Imagery*, p. 240.

4. Pylyshyn, "Imagery and Artificial Intelligence," in Block, *Readings in the Philosophy of Psychology*, vol. 2, p. 177.

5. Ibid., p. 177 and pp. 183–86.

6. Pylyshyn, "The Imagery Debate," p. 165.

7. Thomas Natsoulas, "Haugeland's First Hurdle," *Behavioral and Brain Sciences* 1 (1978): 243; emphasis added.

8. This is not to say, of course, that qualitative states are not affected by beliefs and other sorts of mental representations. Phantom limb pain, hypochondria, and natural childbirth techniques are obvious examples of ways in which qualitative states can have cognitive dimensions. It would not follow, however, that the qualia in question typically function as representations *of* qualities, of the regions in which they are located, or of the beliefs that enhance or diminish them. They could, no doubt, stand for

those things (and others as well: aching joints for coming rain, a flash of yellow for lurking predators). But that is to integrate them into a representational system in a way that is, at best, only minimally dependent on their intrinsic structure and potential for generating new qualia that vary systematically as modes of representation.

9. The problem of qualia is a notorious one for any sort of functionalism. The arguments are too familiar to bear repeating here, but the essential point is that two people who were functionally equivalent in every relevant respect could have entirely different spectra of qualitative experiences. Indeed, one of them could be fully well-organized as a functional type and have no qualia whatsoever. In a functionalist account, the argument says, something must be missing.

A standard response to this argument amounts to a denial of the premises on which it rests. In a narrow sense, pains and other sensory experiences *can* be type individuated by a specification of the roles they play in the production of behavior, in conjunction with other types of mental state. Wherever there is the appropriate sort of functional state, there is a particular kind of pain state. While there might be more to the state than just its functional character, "pain" in some broader sense, whatever more there is simply does not figure into a psychological theory aimed at explaining and predicting behavior. Cf. Sidney Shoemaker, "Functionalism and Qualia," *Philosophical Studies* 27 (1975): 251–67. See also Richard Boyd, "Materialism without Reductionism," in Block, *Readings in the Philosophy of Psychology*, vol. 1, pp. 67–106.

10. Paul Churchland, *Matter and Consciousness* (Cambridge: MIT/Bradford, 1984), p. 40. In this case, qualia could only be absent from, or idiosyncratic to, structures of a sort that are radically different from those that ordinarily perform the relevant sensory function. However, in light of the fact that any one function can be performed by many different structures, explaining phenomenal properties in this way will lead to one of two conclusions: Either those properties actually contribute nothing to the type identity of sensory states and only play a coincidental or supplementary role in the explanation of behavior, or the type identity of sensory states is species-specific. That is, what "pain" is will be determined jointly by function and structure; and its meaning will vary as it occurs in structures of different kinds. Churchland prefers the latter conclusion.

11. Pylyshyn, "Computational Models and Empirical Constraints," *Behavioral and Brain Sciences* 1 (1978): 96.

12. The example comes from Pat Hayes, "Knowing about Formality," *Behavioral and Brain Sciences* 3 (1980): 82.

13. Marvin Minsky, "A Framework for Representing Knowledge," MIT AI Lab Memo 306, 1974, reprinted in Haugeland, *Mind Design*. Roger Schank and Robert P. Ableson, *Scripts, Plans, Goals and Understanding* (Hillsdale, N.J.: Lawrence Erlbaum, 1977); Terry Winograd, "Understanding Natural Language," *Cognitive Psychology* 1 (1972).

14. Bartlett, as quoted in Minsky, "Framework for Representing Knowledge," p. 101. The connection between frames and images requires a bit of extrapolation but is not simply forced. See, for example, Haugeland, *Artificial Intelligence*, pp. 175–230. Haugeland argues that frames are a variant of one type of solution to the frame problem ("how to 'notice' salient side effects" without eliminating all other possibly relevant ones, p. 204). The solution is to employ stereotypes, which are general, conventional descriptions of familiar objects and situations. He thinks visual imagery may provide a better solution: "The beauty of images is that (spatial) side effects take care of themselves" (p. 229). I do not claim, of course, that frames and prototypes just are concrete images. Rather, I want to argue that the representation of typicality that is central to their function is also central to visual imagery and, in some cases, may be better served by it. However, as I will try to show in later sections, how that works, particularly in memory images, is not a simple matter.

15. Hubert Dreyfus, "From Micro-Worlds to Knowledge Representation," in Haugeland, *Mind Design*, p. 185.

16. Quoted in Dreyfus, "From Micro-Worlds to Knowledge Representation," p. 178. See Eleanor Rosch, "Human Categorization," in N. Warren, *Advances in Cross-Cultural Psychology*, vol. 1 (London: Academic Press, 1977), p. 30.

17. Ibid.

18. Hilary Putnam, "Reductionism and the Nature of Psychology," in Haugeland, *Mind Design*, p. 215. This is not to say that Putnam thinks that prototypes or any such thing can be invoked to give an account of the content of mental states. He rejects the view, held at one time by Fodor, that narrow content can be identified with prototypes associated with formulas in mentalese, where a prototype is the output of a pattern recognition module. Putnam argues that such an account will be incomplete, since not every thought or belief will be associated with a prototype. Second, prototypes can vary from one culture to another and so will not be preserved in translation. Thus they cannot account for the narrow content of expressed beliefs. Third, Putnam suggests that prototypes may be unimportant for translation, since the features of a perceptual prototype may omit much of the meaning of terms for the perceived objects. Hence they do not ground the narrow content of beliefs expressed in those terms.

It is important to note that the role I am going to assign prototypes in this and the next chapter is not intended to account for the meaning of expressed beliefs or the narrow content of belief states. Indeed, I will argue that what they do give content to, in certain central cases, cannot be beliefs. Thus Putnam's critique does not apply. A partial theory of narrow content that captures only perceivable properties is just what one wants, to develop an understanding of visual cognition. Whether prototypes actually vary from one context to another I take to be an open empirical question.

Whether they can be of any help at all in establishing narrow content for beliefs is a question I take up in the final chapter. I argue that they can, but the argument depends on a different understanding of prototypes than that of Fodor or Putnam. Putnam says that prototypes cannot be verbal for Fodor's purposes and that images are insufficiently abstract; hence the turn to pattern recognition. I argue that there are several types of image, some of which are stereotypical figures that abstract essential features. Further, there are describable relations among types of image. An account of those relations strengthens the claim that the content of at least some beliefs depends on typical images. See Hilary Putnam, *The Representation of Reality* (Cambridge: MIT/Bradford, 1987), pp. 43–46.

19. Cf. Rosch, "Principles of Categorization," in *Cognition and Categorization*, ed. E. Rosch and B. Lloyd (Hillsdale, N.J.: Lawrence Erlbaum, 1973). There is, as I have noted, some confusion about the status of prototypes. Cf. D. N. Osherson and E. E. Smith, "On the Adequacy of Prototype Theory as a Theory of Concepts," *Cognition* 9 (1981): 35–38.

20. Dreyfus, "From Micro-Worlds to Knowledge Representation," p. 203.

21. John Haugeland, "The Nature and Plausibility of Cognitivism," *Behavioral and Brain Sciences* 1 (1978): 223.

22. Richard Rorty, "A Middle Ground between Neurons and Holograms," *Behavioral and Brain Sciences* 1 (1978): 248.

23. Howard Margolis, *Patterns, Thinking and Cognition* (Chicago: University of Chicago Press, 1982).

24. Gilbert Ryle, *The Concept of Mind* (New York: Barnes and Noble, 1949), p. 247.

25. Ibid., pp. 265ff. Ryle's specific objection to the view that imagining takes a verbal form is that it is a skillful activity that is a matter of "knowing how" and not a matter of propositional knowledge, "knowing that." Further, he rejects descriptions that can be used to refer to something without knowing what sort of thing it is. It is absurd to say, "I see something in my mind's eye, but I cannot make out what sort of thing it is."

Sartre makes a similar point: "If I amuse myself by turning over in my mind the image of a cube, if I pretend that I see its different sides, I shall be no further ahead at the close of the process than I was at the beginning: I have learned nothing." The same holds true for mental descriptions: a sign always retains a certain externality, because, "whether our language is overt or 'internal' . . . it teaches us something." Sartre, *The Psychology of Imagination* (New York: Methuen, 1972), p. 10 and pp. 121–22.

26. Anne Isaac, David Russell, and David Marks, "Imagery and Mental Practice in Trampoline Skill Acquisition," in *Imagery 2*, ed. David Russell, David Marks, and John T. E. Richardson (Dunedan, New Zealand: Human Performance Associates, 1986), pp. 242–45.

27. This is not to deny, of course, that descriptions can provoke very strong emotional reactions. But think of a description of something pro-

vocative of a profound sense of revulsion, fear, anger, desire, compassion, or whatever, and then imagine seeing a vivid, detailed picture of the scene, object, or person so described. Though this may be a matter of individual difference, the comparative force of the picture seems greater, particularly if every verbal embellishment is matched by graphic visual detail.

28. Cf. Cheshire Calhoun and Robert C. Solomon, *What Is an Emotion?* (Oxford: Oxford University Press, 1984), p. 26.

29. Haugeland, "The Nature and Plausibility of Cognitivism," p. 258.

30. See Arthur C. Danto, "Outline of a Theory of Sentential States," *Social Research* 51 (1984). Jerome Bruner, *Actual Minds, Possible Worlds* (Cambridge: Harvard University Press, 1986).

31. Ronald de Sousa, "The Rationality of Emotions," in *Explaining Emotions,* ed. Amelie Oskenberg Rorty (Berkeley: University of California Press, 1980), pp. 142 and 137.

32. Georges Rey, "Functionalism and the Emotions," in *Explaining Emotions,* p. 190.

CHAPTER 4. INTENTIONAL ICONS

1. J. M. Shorter, "Imagination," *Mind* 61 (1952): 536.

2. Ibid., p. 531.

3. Jerry Fodor, *The Language of Thought,* p. 190.

4. Ibid., p. 180.

5. Ibid., p. 183.

6. It is illustrative to contrast Fodor's theory with that of Pylyshyn, to which it bears marked similarities. Pylyshyn argues that the medium for mental representations is essentially a Fregean propositional system, that is, an expressive relation between a function sign and an argument sign ("Imagery and Artificial Intelligence," p. 183). He argues that the purported implicit information contained in pictorial images, which is supposed to distinguish the pictorial from the propositional format, is actually derived from and not discovered in the scene. There is, he maintains, no intrinsic structure in pictures or in what they represent; what constitutes the structure is always entirely a matter of interpretation. And interpretation is defined by a semantic interpretation function that is inherently propositional. In that respect, all the features of an event emerge from the application of interpretation functions appropriate to the task at hand.

However, it is misleading to suggest, as Pylyshyn does, that Fodor's notion of images under descriptions is the same as his own. The issue is whether the image contains any intrinsic organization that explains its capacity to represent. Descriptionalism holds that the image has no intrinsic content whatsoever; its representational capacity is defined by select properties attributed to it under some interpretation. Fodor implies that the image does have its own organization but that it is not sufficiently differentiated to serve a representational function that is viable for cognition: "How the image is taken—what role it plays in cognitive processing—is determined not only by its figural properties, but also by the character of the description it is paired with" (*Language of Thought*, p. 192). That is to say, figural properties are to some extent determinant. The image requires interpretation, but the fact that it has an internal structure imposes limits on the scope of that activity.

7. I take the constraining features here to be functional and formal rather than merely physical. That is, they could be attributed to diverse physico-chemical processes, they combine according to principles, and the combinations are defined relative to semantic properties. What these constrain are functional roles and relations to other representations. In that respect, the argument cannot be simply generalized to get a variety of direct realism, i.e., a claim about how nonrepresentational stimuli from the environment constrain perception.

8. That the elements of the determinate structure constitute a vocabulary depends on showing that what they are used to construct is a representation, the content of which depends on the character of the elements. That point is developed at length in later sections. It should already be clear, however, that the relation between mental displays and mental descriptions is not just internal transduction. The image is the product of transduction and, in some cases, is a representational complement to the description, not just the object of interpretation by it.

9. Dennett, "Two Approaches to Mental Images," in Block, *Imagery*, p. 88. Dennett's critique of mental images, for the most part, has been directed at them as the quintessential inhabitants of consciousness of a traditional sort: introspectable, privileged, and private. Dennett has expressed doubts about the scientific value of the sort of images I am proposing, but he does not insist that they are objectionable altogether. Indeed, there is a sense in which attributing an imagelike function to neural configurations is amenable to his kind of functionalism. This would be particularly true if nonpropositional images were taken to be identifiable in terms of design features of the system. However, any toleration of imagery would be qualified by Dennett's commitment to instrumentalism, particularly insofar as images are said to have psychologically real formal properties and content. For him, beliefs are essentially useful fictions, to be eliminated when possible by a non-intentional psychology of functional states. As information-bearing structures, images would likewise be candidates for elimination.

Dennett has doubts about the ability of representational psychology to overcome problems that result from the need to attribute mental states on the basis of interpretation of behavior. He also argues that attributions of beliefs to people depend on the presupposition of rationality. Hence, it is vacuous, because it assumes what it is supposed to explain. But the fact that a conception of rationality is assumed and spelled out in terms of belief and desire does not vitiate the explanatory status of belief-desire psychology. As an empirical hypothesis, the conception is confirmed or disconfirmed by predictions based on ascribing beliefs and desires. The same would be true for biological design theories, which must presuppose conceptions of fitness and conduciveness to survival. Cf. "Intentional Systems," and "Towards a Cognitive Theory of Consciousness," in Dennett, *Brainstorms.*

10. Fodor, *Language of Thought,* p. 194.

11. Fodor, "Imagistic Representation," p. 77, and Dennett, "The Nature of Images," p. 55, both in Block, *Imagery.*

12. Fodor, *Language of Thought,* p. 190.

13. I do not claim that these are all forms of mental representation but rather that they reinforce the view that depictions are not *generally* reducible to descriptions. And, while there is empirical evidence for some of them (for example, the maplike representations in animals discussed in chapter 6), I am certainly not committed to the simplistic and regressive view that seeing external representations must be explained by internal representations of the same type. The homunculus problem and the regress that it threatens arise for representational psychology generally; and the same appeal to subroutine analysis of the representational function protects pictorialism as much as descriptionalism against it. The mental picture-perception function that might, indeed, contribute to external picture perception is not really perception. Just as it does not simply replicate what it is employed to explain, but is only partly a functional analog, so, too, with the more basic processes that account for it. At some point, references to representational functions of any sort become unnecessary.

14. Goodman, *Languages of Art,* p. 254.

15. Haugeland, "Semantic Engines," in Haugeland, *Mind Design,* p. 22.

16. The notion of "taking care" of content in a wide sense is ambiguous. Fodor does not now think that an account of content comes for free with an understanding of formal relations. Rather, he thinks that an idealized account is required of how mental representation will satisfy truth conditions when functioning properly. Cf. Fodor, *Psychosemantics* (Cambridge: MIT/Bradford, 1987). My analysis here is so far intended to be neutral with respect to several varieties of semantics for psychology, so long as structured internal representations are taken to make some contribution to it.

17. I do not think that, as an interpretive principle, this amounts to assuming a full-blown theory of rationality. It does assume at least minimal rationality of a certain kind; but as noted in footnote 9 above, that is not objectionable. Stich has argued that attributions of belief depend on judgments of similarity rather than a presupposition of rationality, a principle of humanity instead of a principle of charity. Dennett has lately replied

that the two go together. I am going to argue in chap. 6 that imagery plays a role in judgments of similarity, and since I now allow that it assumes some rationality, accepting Dennett's point would seem to lead to a circle: rationality assessments assume similarity judgments, which are themselves identified on the basis of a limited rationality assumption. But the virtue of a pluralistic psychology is that it employs more than one notion of rationality; the different modes can check and reinforce each other in a noncircular way. This point is argued more fully later. Cf. Stich, "Could Man Be an Irrational Animal?," in *Naturalizing Epistemology,* ed. Hilary Kornblith (Cambridge: MIT/Bradford, 1985), pp. 253–60; and Dennett, *The Intentional Stance* (Cambridge: MIT/Bradford, 1987), pp. 339–50.

18. Fodor, "Methodological Solipsism: Replies to Commentators," *Behavioral and Brain Sciences* 3 (1980): 99.

19. Fodor, *Language of Thought,* p. 74n. The sense in which a representational theory is committed to the explicitness of representation is controversial. The controversy is fueled partly by the fact that there are different ways to be explicit. On the notion of canonical form, logical form is explicit, and it "encodes" a "rule," i.e., it exemplifies a standard, which is "implicit" in it: The rule is not itself represented by another representation. Block argues that, insofar as such rules are hardwired, they are implicit and thus not really represented; "Advertisement for Semantics for Psychology," *Midwest Studies in Philosophy* 10 (1986): 640. However, Fodor calls the representation of basic operations and state types explicit, when contrasted with some higher-order rules: "The [higher-order] rules of transformation may, but needn't be explicitly represented. . . . Programs may be explicitly represented and data structures have to be"; "Fodor's Guide to Mental Representation," *Mind* 24 (1985): 94. For my purposes, what matters is that any canonical forms for images be psychologically real and causally efficacious, and that there are higher-order processes, the rules for which may or may not be explicitly represented. Cf. Dennett, *The Intentional Stance,* pp. 215–25, for a fuller discussion.

20. Fodor, "Methodological Solipsism," in *Representations,* p. 227.

21. It is important to note that the computational model actually provides support for that possibility through the principle of the theory-relativity of the symbol identity. The descriptionalist critique simply disregards the applicability of this principle to images.

22. Robert Schwartz, "Imagery—There's More to It Than Meets the Eye," in Block, *Imagery,* pp. 117–21. Schwartz also proposes "to treat imagery as a kind of symbolization" (p. 111); cf. Schwartz, "The Power of Pictures," *Journal of Philosophy* (1985): 711–20. The idea that there are several ways that formal features can be a symbol and that some of the ways overlap supports the use of the term *rule* in describing the principles that govern imagery.

23. Block, "Mental Pictures and Cognitive Science," *Philosophical Review* 92 (1983): 538. Haugeland, *Artificial Intelligence,* pp. 221–30.

24. Block and Bromberger, "States' Rights," *Behavioral and Brain Sciences* 3 (1980): 81.

25. I want to be clear about two points in this regard. First, I do not presuppose here any particular conception of rationality in saying that mental states are identified relative to behavioral norms. See note 17 for a brief discussion of the point. Second, in referring to an agent's taking account of such norms, I do not intend, of course, to make that a condition on all cognition. The point is that we sometimes do behave on the basis of our beliefs about behavioral norms, and that is an important fact that cognitive science ought to be able to explain.

26. Kosslyn and Pomeranz, "Imagery, Propositions, and the Form of Internal Representations," *Cognitive Psychology* 9 (1977), reprinted in Block, *Readings in the Philosophy of Psychology*, vol. 2, p. 154. Kosslyn argues (*Image and Mind*, p. 464) that his theory does not depend upon a simple analogy to perception; and this is true in the sense that images have properties that differ from those of percepts. While not simply an analogy, the point is that the mode of mental representation is similar. Further, Kosslyn argues that for him "a mental image is *not* a picture, but is a depictive representation." Nonetheless, "the fact that images do evince quasi-pictorial properties is a genuine finding." Those properties demand access; thus my analysis is applicable to the theory.

27. See Thomas P. Moran, "The Imprecision of Mental Imagery," *Behavioral and Brain Sciences* 2 (1979): 570.

28. S. Kosslyn, "Medium and Message in Mental Imagery," p. 239.

29. Julian Hochberg, *Perception*, pp. 190–95.

30. Elliot Sober, "Mental Representation," p. 117; Hochberg, *Perception*, pp. 139ff. This is not to say that Gestalt phenomena are not important, in particular, for picture perception. I note certain points of connection to imagery in that regard in later sections. Besides Gestalt psychology, the other alternative to the general approach to perception outlined here is that of Gibson. Initially, Gibson argued that gradients of texture, height, width, and density are defined by perspective compression as a function of distance. These are invariant across changes in the perceiver's location; thus perceptual structure is directly accessible without the need for mental images or higher-order structures. In that respect, the theory is antithetical to the one presented here. In the later theory, Gibson emphasizes higher-order relational information generated by motion. On this approach, edges, corners, and surfaces can be specified by gradients of texture flow velocities or types of discontinuities in the optical flow. As Margaret Hagen argues, the theory seems contradictory with respect to pictures. If perspective pictures contain gradient information, then (since they are single, static views) the purported invariance of such information is irrelevant. If, on the other hand, the perceptual function of the information is really dependent upon its invariance, then gradient information cannot function in singular pic-

tures. The later theory carries the implication that training is required to identify the information in pictures, which capture characteristics of momentary vision; but such is not always the case. Margaret Hagen, "Generative Theory: A Perceptual Theory of Pictorial Representation," in *The Perception of Pictures*, vol. 2, ed. M. Hagen (New York: Academic Press, 1980), p. 22.

31. Richard L. Gregory, "Perceptions as Hypotheses," in *Philosophy of Psychology*, ed. C. Brown (New York: Harper and Row, 1974), p. 203.

32. G. E. M. Anscombe, "Comments on Gregory's Paper," *Philosophy of Psychology*, ed. C. Brown, p. 218.

33. Julian Hochberg, *Perception*, pp. 204–05.

34. Rodolphe Töpffer, *Esai di physiognomie* (Geneva, 1945); *Oeuvres complètes de R. Töpffer*, ed. Pierre Cailler and Henri Daniel (Geneva, 1945), p. 14. See the interesting discussion of "Töpffer's Law" of visual expression in E. Gombrich, *Art and Illusion* (Princeton: Princeton University Press, 1960), pp. 330ff.

35. Cf. Richard Brilliant, *Visual Narratives* (Ithaca: Cornell University Press, 1984), pp. 56–58.

36. It seems especially clear in the case of visual narrative that not only is it irreducible to a set of verbal descriptions but a mere *conjunction* of them with a set of pictures taken to be related by principles of association will not work. Since (a) later stages in the series depend for their formal features on details of the composition of all or a subset of earlier stages and (b) the series can succeed or fail visually, the example lends itself quite well to the notions of visual syntax and semantics.

37. Haugeland, "The Nature and Plausibility of Cognitivism," *Behavioral and Brain Sciences* 1 (1978): 219.

38. The point applies to either conceptual role semantics or to the sort of view that Fodor espouses. These are discussed further in the next chapter.

CHAPTER 5. PROCESS AND CONTENT

1. H. W. Janson, *History of Art*, 2d ed. (New York: Harry N. Abrams, 1979), p. 616. The epigraph's quotation of Fitzgerald is taken from Tony Tanner's introduction to Jane Austen, *Pride and Prejudice* (Harmondsworth: Penguin, 1972), p. 17.

2. The example comes from Arthur Danto, *The Transfiguration of the Commonplace* (Cambridge: Harvard University Press, 1981), p. 36.

3. Haugeland, "Formality and Naturalism," p. 90.

4. See chap. 2, note 29.

5. Fodor, "Fodor's Guide to Mental Representation," pp. 84–89.

6. Block, "Advertisement for Semantics for Psychology," p. 662.

7. If the standard conception of both symbol structures and abstractable

functions should prove to be wrong, of course, then imaging will not be as I have described it here. To put it more congenially, some of the interesting properties of imagery will carry over, and it will be controversial whether the explanation of them in terms of the implementation of visual norms or rules will provide a useful research and predictive strategy. See note 23 in chap. 1 for my reservation about connectionist claims in that regard.

8. Cf. Julian Hochberg and Virginia Brooks, "Pictorial Recognition as an Unlearned Ability," *American Journal of Psychology* 75 (1962): 624–28.

9. Danto, "Depiction and Description," p. 11.

10. D. J. O'Connor and Brian Carr, *Introduction to Theory of Knowledge* (Minneapolis: University of Minnesota Press, 1982), pp. 111–15.

11. Paul Churchland, *Matter and Consciousness*, pp. 63–66. Cf. Churchland, "Eliminative Materialism and Propositional Attitudes," *Journal of Philosophy* 78 (1978), sec. 1.

12. Marcel Proust, "Within a Budding Grove," *Remembrance of Things Past*, trans. C. K. Scott Moncrieff (New York: Random House, 1982), p. 1009.

13. If even this reading seems too intellectualist, see Tanner's introduction to Austen, *Pride and Prejudice*. He argues that Austen's work was influenced by British empiricism, an influence made palpable in scenes where the protagonist reflects upon a portrait and, in discovering certain features, has her beliefs confirmed or disconfirmed. She thus learns about the character of her own "ideas" and images, a prelude to changing them. Austen apparently studied Gainsborough portraits for *types* but could find none for Darcy. One could argue that there is evidence in the text of a theory of representational types and their relation to originality and individuality. In part the evidence is the text itself, which has a stereotypical ending. Austen has been criticized for that, but a case can be made that the ending makes a point about the essential connection of particular creative representation to the type from which it deviates.

14. Of six general types of pictorial representation theory, three either involve perception in an essential way or carry significant implications concerning it. They are theories of resemblance, illusion, and information. The other three—convention theory, causal history accounts, and theories of the producer's intention—need not invoke or imply specifically a perceptual psychology. If having an image is like seeing a picture in some way, then the role of intention and (internal) cause can be relevant, but not necessarily so as to require invoking particular theories of pictorial representation of this sort. Neither resemblance nor convention provide necessary or sufficient conditions for pictorial representation; and as previous arguments regarding isomorphism and canonical form should make clear, they also cannot serve as accounts for mental imagery.

Although the notion of "information" seems highly amenable to a cognitivist theory of mental imagery, the term is notoriously ambiguous. Originally, the emphasis was on specifying informational content quantitatively, in terms of degree of uncertainty reduction in a signal. In that form, the character of the stimulus and the particular "meaning" or content of the signal are irrelevant. This "syntactic" account of the improbability of the occurrence of a state contrasts with a "semantic" information theory. On that account, informational content is specified in terms of epistemic probability, i.e., the improbability of the truth of a hypothesis.

While the syntactic version of this theory bears some resemblance to a model of representations individuated formally, it is clear that what is important for that model is the semantic capacities of those forms defined by their role in rule-governed procedures. These are not concerned exclusively with occurrence-frequencies of incoming signals. Semantic information theory is explicitly invoked by Gombrich in *Art and Illusion* and by Elliot Sober, "Mental Representation," *Synthese* 33 (1976), as relevant to the psychology of pictorial representation. However, its applicability, for Sober at least, is clearly dependent upon construing pictures as impoverished linguistic systems, a reduction which he admits is merely an approximation in many cases. In order to use the theory it is necessary to treat a picture as a statement from which a reader could learn as much as a perceiver could from the picture. But as Max Black notes, "A picture shows more than can be said" ("How Do Pictures Represent?" p. 109). As Black points out, the moral of information theory is that information is relative to a body of knowledge. Yet it remains an open question whether the representation of that knowledge is necessarily linguistic in form.

15. Hochberg, "Pictorial Functions and Perceptual Structures," p. 74; see also pp. 58–59. Cf. Hochberg, *Perception,* p. 195.

16. Hochberg, *Perception,* p. 195.

17. Cf. Haugeland, *Mind Design,* pp. 15ff; Pylyshyn, *Computation and Cognition,* p. 78.

18. Kosslyn, et al., "On the Demystification of Imagery," p. 133. Cf. Dennett, "The Nature of Images," p. 54. See also the discussion of the concept in chap. 1 above, and Richard Wollheim, *Art and Its Objects* (Cambridge: Cambridge University Press, 1980), sec. 11–14; and Roger Scruton, *Art and Imagination,* chaps. 7 and 8.

19. Ludwig Wittgenstein, *Philosophical Investigations,* p. 213.

20. Ibid., p. 193. Cf. Hide Ishiguro, "Imagination," *Proceedings of the Aristotelean Society,* supp. vol. 61 (1967), p. 44. In the case of representational entities, there are two objects of sight, the physical object identified in nonrepresentational terms—lines on paper or paint on canvas—and a representation—a sketch or portrait. The latter is defined by an "internal relation between it and other objects," so that whenever something is seen as a representation, it is necessarily seen as a representation of another thing. The physical object is identified by external relations, a description of which would typically invoke the causal ancestry of the object.

21. Ishiguro, "Imagination," p. 54.

22. Cf. Wollheim, *Art and Its Objects*, p. 213.

23. That is not to say, of course, that degree of acceptance can be assimilated to the frequency of the occurrence of a visual or verbal hypothesis, or that it is necessarily the result of repeated input. Relations to other attitudes affect acceptance. The point is just that having an attitude, taken as being generally dependent on relations among representations, is a condition on establishing the epistemic function of any one of them.

CHAPTER 6. IMAGERY ON THE BOUNDS OF COGNITION

1. Brian Loar, "Syntax, Functional Semantics, and Referential Semantics," *Behavioral and Brain Sciences* 3 (1980).

2. Paul Churchland, "In Defense of Naturalism," p. 75.

3. The term *notional array* belongs to Dan Lloyd, "Picturing," unpublished Ph.D. dissertation, Columbia University (1982). His use of notionality, however, is closer to Dennett's and is not committed to a particular mode of psychological reality.

4. The classic articles are Putnam, "The Meaning of Meaning," in *Mind, Language, and Reality: Philosophical Papers*, vol. 2 (1979); Tyler Burge, "Individualism and the Mental," *Midwest Studies in Philosophy* 4 (1979): 73–121.

5. Cf. Fodor, "Cognitive Science and the Twin-Earth Problem," pp. 98–122, and "Observation Reconsidered," *Philosophy of Science* 51 (1989): 23–43. Fodor's present view is somewhat different than this. See *Psychosemantics* (Cambridge: MIT/Bradford, 1987) and "Banish DisContent," in *Language, Mind, and Logic*, ed. J. Butterfield (Cambridge: Cambridge University Press, 1986).

6. Even with the possibility of identifying productive relations among prototypes and other types of image, such an account of content will be only partial. See note 18, chap. 3, for a brief discussion of Putnam's argument in this regard and my argument that the critique does not apply to the theory of imagery developed here.

7. Putnam, "Reductionism and the Nature of Psychology," pp. 205–19.

8. Stich, *From Folk Psychology to Cognitive Science*, chap. 7.

9. Ibid., p. 79.

10. Ibid., p. 147.

11. Cf. Robert Goldstein, Larry C. Walrath, John A. Stern, and Barbara Strock, "Blink Activity in a Discrimination Task," *Psychophysiology* 22 (1985). The authors are not committed, of course, to my interpretation of their results.

12. Stich, *From Folk Psychology to Cognitive Science*, pp. 54–56. The case is that of Mrs. T., who loses her ability to answer questions about a

belief that she continues to assert, viz., that McKinley was assassinated. Stich argues that, on the content theory of belief, it is not clear whether her belief is the same as that of a fully functional person.

13. Cf. Richard Nisbett and Lee Ross, "Judgmental Heuristics and Knowledge Structures," in *Naturalizing Epistemology*, ed. Hilary Kornblith (Cambridge: MIT/Bradford, 1985), pp. 189–216.

14. See, for example, Sartre, *Psychology of Imagination*, p. 13. Cf. Donald A. Schon, "Generative Metaphor: A Perspective on Problem-Setting in Social Policy," in *Metaphor and Thought*, ed. A. Ortony, p. 255.

15. David Lewis, "Attitudes De Dicto and De Se," *Philosophical Review* 88 (1979): 529.

16. Roger Scruton, *Art and Imagination*, p. 99.

17. Ibid., p. 109.

18. Ibid., p. 115.

19. Fodor, *Language of Thought*, pp. 28–31.

20. Ibid., p. 158. See also the last chapter of *Representations*, "The Present Status of the Innateness Controversy," in which Fodor's reservations about exemplars and prototypes are expressed even more strongly.

21. H. L. Roitblatt, "The Meaning of Representation in Animal Memory," *Behavioral and Brain Sciences* 5 (1982): 397.

22. Danto, "Behaviorism's New Cognitive Representations: Paradigm Regained," p. 375. Cf. Nadel, "Some Thoughts on the Proper Foundations for the Study of Cognition in Animals," p. 353.

23. S. Suzuki, G. Augerinos, and A. H. Black, "Stimulus Control of Spatial Behavior on the Eight-arm Maze in Rats," *Learning and Motivation* 11 (1980): 1–18. Roitblatt argues in favor of lists, which nonetheless "intrinsically" code order ("The Meaning of Representation in Animal Memory," p. 361).

24. Herbert Terrace, "On the Nature of Animal Thinking," *Neuroscience and Biobehavioral Reviews* 9 (1985): 643–52; "In the Beginning Was the 'Name,'" *American Psychologist* 40 (1985): 1011.

25. Wollheim, *Art and Its Objects*, p. 216.

26. For a different use of the idea of metarepresentation, see Dan Lloyd, *Simple Minds* (Cambridge: MIT/Bradford, 1989). On his account, the representation that is the object of mental representation is external to the mind.

27. Hochberg, "The Representation of Things and People," pp. 91, 88.

28. Cf. Lewis, "Attitudes De Dicto and De Se," who argues for treating attitude ascription in terms of states or properties of persons (p. 539). Cf. Thomas Nagel, "The Boundaries of Inner Space," *Journal of Philosophy* 65 (1969).

Bibliography

Anderson, John R. "Arguments Concerning Representations for Mental Imagery." *Psychological Review* 85 (1978).

Anscombe, G. E. M. "Comments on Gregory's Paper." In *Philosophy of Psychology*, edited by C. Brown. New York: Harper and Row, 1974.

Aune, Bruce. "Comments on 'Psychological Predicates.'" In *Art, Mind, and Religion*, edited by W. H. Capitan and D. D. Merrill. Pittsburgh: University of Pittsburgh Press, 1967.

Berkeley, George. *An Essay toward a New Theory of Vision.* In *Berkeley's Philosophical Writings*, edited by David M. Armstrong. Toronto: Collier-Macmillan, 1965.

Black, Max. "How Do Pictures Represent?" In *Art, Perception, and Reality*, edited by Maurice Mandelbaum. Baltimore: Johns Hopkins University Press, 1970.

Block, Ned. "Advertisement for Semantics for Psychology." *Midwest Studies in Philosophy* 10 (1986): 640.

———. "Mental Pictures and Cognitive Science." *Philosophical Review* 92 (1983).

———, ed. *Readings in the Philosophy of Psychology*, vols. 1 and 2. Cambridge: Harvard University Press, 1980–81.

———. *Imagery.* Cambridge: MIT/Bradford, 1981.

Block, Ned, and Sylvain Bromberger. "States' Rights." *Behavioral and Brain Sciences* 3 (1980).

Block, Ned, and Jerry Fodor. "What Psychological States Are Not." *Philosophical Review* 81 (1972).

Boyd, Richard. "Materialism without Reductionalism: What Physicalism Does Not Entail." In Ned Block, *Readings in the Philosophy of Psychology*, vol. 1.

Brown, R., and R. J. Herrnstein. "Icons and Images." In Ned Block, *Imagery*.

Bruner, Jerome. *Actual Minds, Possible Worlds.* Cambridge: Harvard University Press, 1986.

Burge, Tyler. "Individualism and the Mental." *Midwest Studies in Philosophy* 4 (1979).

Calhoun, Cheshire, and Robert C. Solomon, eds. *What Is an Emotion?* Oxford: Oxford University Press, 1984.

Carterette, Edward C., and Morton P. Friedman, eds. *The Handbook of Perception,* 10 vols. New York: Academic Press, 1976–80.

Casey, Edward S. *Imagining.* Bloomington: Indiana University Press, 1976.

Chomsky, Noam. *Language and Mind.* New York: Harcourt, 1968.

———. "Rules and Representations." *Behavioral and Brain Sciences* 3 (1980).

Churchland, Patricia Smith. *Neurophilosophy.* Cambridge: MIT, 1986.

———. "A Perspective on Mind-Brain Research." *Journal of Philosophy* 77 (1980).

Churchland, Paul. "Eliminative Materialism and Propositional Attitudes." *Journal of Philosophy* 78 (1981).

———. *Matter and Consciousness.* Cambridge: MIT/Bradford, 1984.

———. "Plasticity: Conceptual and Neuronal." *Behavioral and Brain Sciences* 3 (1980).

Cooper, Lynn. "Modeling the Mind's Eye." *Behavioral and Brain Sciences* 2 (1979).

Danto, Arthur C. "Behaviorism's New Cognitive Representations: Paradigm Regained." *Behavioral and Brain Sciences* 5 (1982).

———. "Concerning Mental Pictures." *Journal of Philosophy* 55 (1958).

———. "Depiction and Description." *Philosophy and Phenomenological Research* 43 (1982).

———. "Outline of a Theory of Sentential States." *Social Research* 51 (1984).

———. "Representational Properties and Mind-Body Identity." *Review of Metaphysics* 26 (1973).

———. *The Transfiguration of the Commonplace.* Cambridge: Harvard University Press, 1981.

Dennett, Daniel C. *Brainstorms: Philosophical Essays on Mind and Psychology.* Cambridge: MIT/Bradford, 1981.

———. *Content and Consciousness.* London: Routledge and Kegan Paul, 1969.

———. "Co-opting Holograms." *Behavioral and Brain Sciences* 1 (1978).

———. "A Cure for the Common Code." In Dennett, *Brainstorms.*

———. *The Intentional Stance.* Cambridge: MIT/Bradford, 1987.

———. "The Nature of Images." In Block, *Imagery.*

De Sousa, Ronald. "The Rationality of Emotions." In *Explaining Emotions,* ed. Amelie O. Rorty. Berkeley: University of California Press, 1980.

Dilman, Ilman. "Imagination." *Proceedings of the Aristotelean Society,* suppl. vol. 61, 1967.

Dretske, Fred. *Knowledge and the Flow of Information.* Cambridge: MIT/Bradford, 1984.

Dreyfus, Hubert. "From Micro-Worlds to Knowledge Representation." In

Mind Design, edited by John Haugeland. Cambridge: MIT/Bradford, 1982.

Enc, Berent. "In Defense of the Identity Theory." *Journal of Philosophy* 80 (1983).

Fisher, John, ed. *Perceiving Artworks*. Philadelphia: Temple University Press, 1980.

Fodor, Jerry A. "The Appeal to Tacit Knowledge in Psychological Explanation." *Journal of Philosophy* 65 (1968).

———. "Banish DisContent." In J. Butterfield, *Language, Mind, and Logic*. Cambridge: Cambridge University Press, 1986.

———. "Cognitive Science and the Twin-Earth Problem." *Notre Dame Journal of Formal Logic* 23 (1982).

———. "Fodor's Guide to Mental Representation." *Mind* 24 (1985).

———. "Imagistic Representation." In Block, *Imagery*.

———. *The Language of Thought*. New York: Crowell, 1975.

———. "Methodological Solipsism: Replies to Commentators." *Behavioral and Brain Sciences* 3 (1980).

———. *The Modularity of Mind*. Cambridge: MIT/Bradford, 1983.

———. "Observation Reconsidered." *Philosophy of Science* 51 (1989).

———. *Psychological Explanation: An Introduction to the Philosophy of Psychology*. New York: Random House, 1968.

———. *Psychosemantics*. Cambridge: MIT/Bradford, 1987.

———. *Representations: Philosophical Essays on the Foundations of Cognitive Science*. Cambridge: MIT/Bradford, 1981.

Gibson, James J. *The Ecological Approach to Visual Perception*. Boston: Houghton Mifflin, 1979.

———. *The Senses Considered as Perceptual Systems*. Boston: Houghton Mifflin, 1976.

Goldman, Alvin. "A Causal Theory of Knowing." *Journal of Philosophy* 64 (1967).

Gombrich, Ernst. *Art and Illusion*. Princeton: Princeton University Press, 1969.

———. "The Mask and the Face: The Perception of Physiognomic Likeness in Life and in Art." In *Art, Perception, and Reality*, edited by Maurice Mandelbaum. Baltimore: Johns Hopkins University Press, 1970.

Goodman, Nelson. *The Languages of Art*. 2d ed. Indianapolis: Hackett, 1976.

Gregory, Richard. "Perceptions as Hypotheses." In *Philosophy of Psychology*, edited by C. Brown. New York: Harper and Row, 1974.

Hagen, Margaret. "Generative Theory: A Perceptual Theory of Pictorial Representation." In *The Perception of Pictures*, vol. 2, edited by Margaret Hagen. New York: Academic Press, 1980.

Hannay, Alastair. *Mental Images: A Defence*. Atlantic Highlands, N.J.: Humanities Press, 1971.

Harmon, Gilbert. *Thought.* Princeton: Princeton University Press, 1973.

Haugeland, John. *Artificial Intelligence: The Very Idea.* Cambridge: MIT/Bradford, 1985.

————. "Formality and Naturalism." *Behavioral and Brain Sciences* 3 (1980).

————. "The Nature and Plausibility of Cognitivism." *Behavioral and Brain Sciences* 1 (1978).

————. "Psychology and Computational Architecture." *Behavioral and Brain Sciences* 3 (1980).

————, ed. *Mind Design.* Cambridge: MIT/Bradford, 1982.

Hayes, Pat. "Knowing about Formality." *Behavioral and Brain Sciences* 3 (1980).

Hebb, D. O. *The Organization of Behavior.* New York: Wiley, 1949.

Hochberg, Julian. "Organization and the Gestalt Tradition." In *The Handbook of Perception,* vol. 1, edited by Edward C. Carterette and Morton P. Friedman. New York: Academic Press, 1978.

————. *Perception.* 2d ed. Englewood Cliffs, N.J.: Prentice-Hall, 1978.

————. "Perception: Towards the Recovery of a Definition." *Psychological Review* 63 (1956).

————. "Pictorial Functions and Perceptual Structures." In *The Perception of Pictures,* vol. 2, edited by Margaret Hagen. New York: Academic Press, 1980.

————. "The Representation of Things and People." In *Art, Perception, and Reality,* edited by Maurice Mandelbaum. Baltimore: Johns Hopkins University Press, 1970.

Hochberg, Julian, and Virginia Brooks. "Pictorial Recognition as an Unlearned Ability: A Study of One Child's Performance." *American Journal of Psychology* 73 (1960).

Hornstein, Norbert. "Review of Philosophical Perspectives on Artificial Intelligence." *Journal of Philosophy* 77 (1980).

Howard, I. P. "Recognition and Knowledge of the Water-Level Principle." *Perception* 7 (1978).

Howell, Robert. "Ordinary Pictures, Mental Representations, and Logical Forms." *Synthese* 33 (1976).

Ishiguro, Hide. "Imagination." In *British Analytic Philosophy,* edited by Bernard Williams and Alan Montefiore. London: Routledge and Kegan Paul, 1966.

————. "Imagination." *Proceedings of the Aristotelean Society,* supp. vol. 61, 1967.

Kalke, William. "What is Wrong with Fodor and Putnam's Functionalism." *Nous* 3 (1969).

Katz, Jerrold. "Fodor's Guide to Cognitive Psychology." *Behavioral and Brain Sciences* 3 (1980).

Kaufman, Lloyd. *Sight and Mind.* New York: Oxford University Press, 1974.

Kohler, Wolfgang. *Gestalt Psychology*. New York: Liveright, 1947.

Kosslyn, Stephen M. *Ghosts in the Mind's Machine*. New York: Norton, 1983.

———. *Image and Mind*. Cambridge: Harvard University Press, 1980.

———. "The Medium and the Message in Mental Imagery." In Block, *Imagery*.

Kosslyn, Stephen M., and Gary Hatfield. "Representation without Symbol Systems." In *Social Research* 51 (1984).

Kosslyn, Stephen M., S. Pinker, G. E. Smith, and S. P. Schwartz, "On the Demystification of Mental Imagery." *Behavioral and Brain Sciences* 2 (1979). Reprinted in Block, *Imagery*.

Kosslyn, Stephen M., and J. R. Pomeranz. "Imagery, Propositions, and the Form of Internal Representations." *Cognitive Psychology* 9 (1977). Reprinted in Block, *Readings in the Philosophy of Psychology*, vol. 2.

Lewis, David. "An Argument for the Identity Theory." In *Materialism and the Mind-Body Problem*, edited by David Rosenthal. Englewood Cliffs, N.J.: Prentice-Hall, 1971.

———. "Attitudes De Dicto and De Se." *Philosophical Review* 88 (1979).

———. Review of *Art, Mind, and Religion*, edited by W. H. Capitan and D. D. Merrill. *Journal of Philosophy* 66 (1969).

Lloyd, Dan. "Picturing." Ph.D. diss., Columbia University, 1982.

———. *Simple Minds*. Cambridge: MIT/Bradford, 1989.

Loar, Brian. "Syntax, Functional Semantics, and Referential Semantics." *Behavioral and Brain Sciences* 3 (1980).

Mandelbaum, Maurice, ed. *Art, Perception, and Reality*. Baltimore: Johns Hopkins University Press, 1970.

Margolis, Howard. *Patterns, Thinking and Cognition*. Chicago: University of Chicago Press, 1982.

Marr, David and H. Keith Nishihara. "Visual Information Processing: Artificial Intelligence and the Sensorium of Sight." *Technology Review* 81 (October 1978).

Matthews, Robert J. "Troubles with Representationalism." *Social Research* 51 (1984).

Miller, George A., Eugene Galanter, and Karl H. Pribram. *Plans and the Structure of Behavior*. New York: Holt, Rinehart and Winston, 1960.

Minsky, Marvin. "A Framework for Representing Knowledge." In *Mind Design*, edited by John Haugeland. Cambridge: MIT/Bradford, 1982.

Moran, Thomas P. "The Imprecision of Mental Imagery." *Behavioral and Brain Sciences* 2 (1979).

Morgenbesser, Sidney. "Fodor on Ryle." *Journal of Philosophy* 66 (1969).

Nadel, L. "Some Thoughts on the Proper Foundations for the Study of Cognition in Animals." *Behavioral and Brain Sciences* 5 (1982).

Nagel, Thomas. "The Boundaries of Inner Space." *Journal of Philosophy* 66 (1969).

Natsoulas, Thomas. "Haugeland's First Hurdle." *Behavioral and Brain Sciences* 1 (1978).

Neisser, Ulrich. *Cognition and Reality.* San Francisco: Freeman, 1976.

Nelson, R. J. "Mechanism, Functionalism, and the Identity Theory." *Journal of Philosophy* 73 (1976).

Newell, A., and H. Simon. *Human Problem Solving.* Englewood Cliffs, N.J.: Prentice-Hall, 1972.

Nisbett, Richard, and Lee Ross. "Judgmental Heuristics and Knowledge Structures." In *Naturalizing Epistemology,* edited by Hilary Kornblith. Cambridge: MIT/Bradford, 1985.

Nodine, Calvin, and and Dennis Fisher, eds. *Perception and Pictorial Representation.* New York: Praeger, 1979.

Ortony, A., ed. *Metaphor and Thought.* Cambridge: Cambridge University Press, 1979.

Osherson, D. N., and E. E. Smith. "On the Adequacy of Prototype Theory as a Theory of Concepts." *Cognition* 9 (1981).

Paivio, Allan. *Imagery and Verbal Processes.* New York: Holt, Rinehart and Winston, 1971.

Perky, C. W. "An Experimental Study of Imagination." *American Journal of Psychology* 21 (1910).

Pinker, Steven. "Explanations in Theories of Language and of Imagery." *Behavioral and Brain Sciences* 3 (1980).

Place, U. T. "Comments on Putnam's 'Psychological Predicates.'" In *Art, Mind, and Religion,* edited by W. H. Capitan and D. D. Merrill. Pittsburgh: University of Pittsburgh Press, 1967.

Plato. *Protagoras.* Translated by W. K. Guthrie. Harmondsworth: Penguin, 1956.

Pucetti, Roland "Are Right Hemisphere Activities Cognitivistic?" *Behavioral and Brain Sciences* 1 (1978).

Putnam, Hilary. *Meaning and the Moral Sciences.* London: Routledge and Kegan Paul, 1978.

———. "The Mental Life of Some Machines." In *Intentionality, Minds, and Perception,* edited by Hector-Neri Casteneda. Detroit: Wayne State University Press, 1967.

———. *Mind, Language, and Reality: Philosophical Papers,* vol. 2. Cambridge: Cambridge University Press, 1975.

———. "Minds and Machines." In *Dimensions of Mind,* edited by Sidney Hook. New York: Collier Books, 1960.

———. "Psychological Predicates." In *Materialism and the Mind-Body Problem,* edited by David Rosenthal. Englewood Cliffs, N.J.: Prentice-Hall, 1971.

———. "Reductionism and the Nature of Psychology." in Haugeland, *Mind Design.*

———. *The Representation of Reality.* Cambridge: MIT/Bradford, 1987.

Pylyshyn, Zenon. "Computation and Cognition." *Behavioral and Brain Sciences* 3 (1980).

———. *Computation and Cognition: Toward a Foundation for Cognitive Science.* 2d ed. Cambridge: MIT/Bradford, 1985.

———. "Computational Models and Empirical Constraints." *Behavioral and Brain Sciences* 1 (1978).

———. "Imagery and Artificial Intelligence." In Block, *Readings in the Philosophy of Psychology*, vol. 2.

———. "The Imagery Debate." In Block, *Imagery*.

———. "Imagery Theory." *Behavioral and Brain Sciences* 2 (1979).

Rey, Georges. "The Formal and the Opaque." *Behavioral and Brain Sciences* 3 (1980).

———. "Functionalism and the Emotions." In *Explaining Emotions*, edited by Amelie Oskenberg Rorty. Berkeley: University of California Press, 1980.

———. "What Are Mental Images?" In Block, *Readings in the Philosophy of Psychology*, vol. 2.

Roitblatt, H. L. "The Meaning of Representation in Animal Memory." *Behavioral and Brain Sciences* 5 (1982).

Rorty, Richard. "A Middle Ground between Neurons and Holograms." *Behavioral and Brain Sciences* 1 (1978).

Rosch, Eleanor. "Human Categorization." In *Advances in Cross-Cultural Psychology*, vol. 1, edited by N. Warren. London: Academic Press, 1977.

Rosch, E., and B. Lloyd, eds. *Cognition and Categorization.* Hillsdale, N.J.: Lawrence Erlbaum, 1973.

Rosenthal, David. *Materialism and the Mind-Body Problem.* Englewood Cliffs, N.J.: Prentice-Hall, 1971.

Ryle, Gilbert. *The Concept of Mind.* New York: Barnes and Noble, 1949.

Sartre, Jean Paul. *Imagination: A Psychological Critique.* Translated by Forrest Williams. Ann Arbor: University of Michigan, 1972.

———. *The Psychology of Imagination.* New York: Methuen, 1972.

Schon, Donald A. "Generative Metaphor: A Perspective on Problem-Setting in Social Policy." In Ortony, *Metaphor and Thought*.

Schwartz, Robert. "Imagery—There's More To It Than Meets the Eye." In Block, *Imagery*.

———. "The Power of Pictures." *Journal of Philosophy* 82 (1985).

———. "Some Limits and Problems of Cognitivism." *Behavioral and Brain Sciences* 1 (1978).

Scruton, Roger. *Art and Imagination.* London: Routledge and Kegan Paul, 1974.

Searle, John. *Minds, Brains, and Science.* Cambridge: Harvard University Press, 1984.

———. "Two Objections to Methodological Solipsism," In *Behavioral and Brain Sciences* 3 (1980).

Shepard, R. N. "Form, Formation, and Transformation of Internal Representation." In *Contemporary Issues in Cognitive Psychology*, edited by R. Solso. Washington: Winston & Sons, 1973.

———. "The Mental Image." *American Psychologist* 33 (1978).

Shepard, R. N., and Lynn Cooper. *Mental Images and Their Transformations*. Cambridge: MIT/Bradford, 1986.

Shepard, R. N., and S. Chipman. "Second-order Isomorphism of Internal Representations: Shapes of States." *Cognitive Psychology* 1 (1970).

Shoemaker, Sidney. "Functionalism and Qualia." *Philosophical Studies* 27 (1975).

Shorter, J. M. "Imagination." *Mind* 61 (1952).

Simon, H. A. "What Is Visual Imagery? An Information Processing Interpretation." In *Cognition in Learning and Memory*, edited by L. W. Gregg. New York: John Wiley, 1972.

Smart, J. J. C. "Sensations and Brain Processes." *Philosophical Review* 68 (1959).

Sober, Elliot. "Mental Representation." *Synthese* 33 (1976).

Solso, R., ed. *Contemporary Issues in Cognitive Psychology*. Washington: Winston & Sons, 1973.

Sterelny, Kim. "The Imagery Debate." In *Philosophy of Science* 53 (1986).

Stich, Stephen. "Autonomous Psychology and the Belief-Desire Thesis." *The Monist* 61 (1978).

———. "Could Man Be an Irrational Animal?" In *Naturalizing Epistemology*, edited by Hilary Kornblith. Cambridge: MIT/Bradford, 1985.

———. *From Folk Psychology to Cognitive Science: The Case against Belief*. Cambridge: MIT/Bradford, 1987.

Strawson, P. F. *The Bounds of Sense*. London: Methuen, 1966.

Suzuki, S., G. Augerinos, and A. H. Black. "Stimulus Control of Spatial Behavior on the Eight-arm Maze in Rats." *Learning and Motivation* 11 (1980).

Taylor, Charles. *The Explanation of Behavior*. London: Routledge and Paul, 1964.

Terrace, Herbert. "In the Beginning Was the 'Name.'" *American Psychologist* 40 (1985).

———. "On the Nature of Animal Thinking." *Neuroscience and Biobehavioral Review* 9 (1985).

Tye, Michael. "The Debate about Mental Imagery." *Journal of Philosophy* 81 (1984).

Von Neumann, J. *Theory of Self-Reproducing Automata*. Edited by A. W. Burks. Urbana: University of Illinois Press, 1966.

Winograd, Terry. "Understanding Natural Language." *Cognitive Psychology* 1 (1972).

Wittgenstein, Ludwig. *Philosophical Investigations*. Translated by G. E. M. Anscombe. New York: Macmillan, 1958.

Wollheim, Richard. *Art and Its Objects.* Cambridge, Eng.: Cambridge University Press, 1980.

———. *On Art and the Mind.* Cambridge: Harvard University Press, 1963.

Yevick, Miriam L. "The Two Modes of Identifying Objects." *Behavioral and Brain Sciences* 1 (1978).

Yuille, John C. "The Crisis in Theories of Mental Imagery." In *Imagery, Memory, and Cognition: Essays in Honor of Allan Paivio,* edited by John C. Yuille. Hillsdale, N.J.: Lawrence Erlbaum, 1983.

Index

Access relations: functional patterns and, 13–14; kinds of, 127–28

Aesthetic psychology, xv, xvi, 59–60

Ambiguity, 114–17

Analog, as term, 74

Analogical thinking, 122

Analog process, 25–26, 28–30, 45; composition and, 74–75; operations on images and, 22; visual narrative and, 84

Animal cognition, 108, 121–27

Anscombe, Elizabeth, 80

Appropriateness, imagery as reasoning in terms of, 122–23

Appropriateness conditions, 72; characteristic image and, 131; on emotions, 60–61; on mapping, 126; nonpropositional representations and, 70–76; provisional images and, 107

Array model, 22–25, 36, 47–48

Artificial intelligence, 46–47, 51, 137n16

Artistic expression, 101, 130

Attitudes: *de dicto vs. de re* distinction and, 113–14; forms of, 95, 115–16; relation between narrow and wide senses of, 117–18; sentential vs. pictorial modes of representation for, 127–29. *See also* Nonpropositional attitudes; Pictorial attitudes; Propositional attitudes

Austen, Jane, *Pride and Prejudice*, 98–99

Autonomy, the principle of. *See* Formality condition

Autonomy of psychology, 4

Bartlett, F. C., 51

Basic pictures, 91

Belief-ascribing sentences, 128–29

Belief attribution, 114

Beliefs, 5; animals and, 122–24; content of, 10, 48; *de dicto vs. de re*, 112–16; dual relation in attribution of, 119; elimination of, 118–19; externalist theory and, 9–10; formal representation and, 10; image recognition and, 116; image rotation and, 87–88; imagery and, 23–25; patterns in visual series and, 94; perceptual, 48; pictorial attitudes and, 96; prototypes and, 141n18; representational competence and, 93; revision of, 99; theories of emotion and, 58. *See also* Propositional attitudes

Binary code, 11–12

Black, Max, 150n14

Block, Ned, 75, 89, 133n6, 146n19

British empiricism, 20–21, 149n13

Bruner, Jerome, 59

Canonical form, 72–74, 78, 101, 130, 149n19. *See also* Schema

Categorization, 51, 52–53

Causal relations, 26–27, 28, 30, 90